BACK TO
THIRTEEN STATES

BACK TO

THIRTEEN STATES

by

JOHN STAFFORD BROWN

VANTAGE PRESS

New York   Washington   Hollywood

PREFACE

This suggested plan for the reorganization of the United States to meet, if possible, some of the seemingly endless emergencies of the present socio-political situation is not by any means—as the title may, perhaps with deliberate provocativeness, imply—a plea for a return to the horse-and-buggy days. Far from it! It is, however, the essence of a lifetime of observation stretching, literally, from the horse-and-buggy days to the era of the supersonic transport; a lifetime spent productively in the heat and fury of the pell-mell development of the nation's natural resources, followed by a decade of leisurely reflection over the often ghastly results of this exploitation.

The ideas advanced in the ensuing pages took form in this last decade and were set down in a preliminary version in the winter of 1969-70, shortly before the mild stir produced by publication of the so-called Tugwell constitution.[1] Perusal of this document leaves the writer pretty much in agreement with columnist James Kilpatrick (*Baltimore Sun*, Dec. 1, 1970) that it is hardly worth discussing. However, it does signify some of the political ferment now permeating the land; and it is interesting, specifically, with reference to the present proposition in that it suggests vaguely the reorganization of the United States into a much smaller number of "republics," not exceeding twenty in all, at least for the coterminal area in North America.

In the present exposition the author sets forth in detail a proposal for reconstructing this coterminal heartland into

---

1. *The Center Magazine*, Santa Barbara, Cal., Sept.-Oct. 1970, pp. 25-45.

thirteen superstates engineered to conform to natural units of drainage, but adjusted in some degree to fit climatic variations, and tailored to accommodate regional desires and necessities. It is his belief that effectuation of this or some reasonably similar plan would simplify many governmental problems, facilitate decentralization of the unwieldy bureaucracy now concentrated in the hands of the Federal Government, and permit the return of these functions and their support, or elimination, to the regions and localities in which they are exercised, thus placing responsibility much closer to the people. This is a course currently being advocated by President Nixon, as set forth in his State of the Nation address (Jan. 22, 1971), but which, under our present political structure, based on fifty jealous and divergent statehoods, seems to have small chance of winning any substantial degree of acceptance.

ACKNOWLEDGMENTS

The author is indebted to various friends and relatives for encouragement in the preparation of this work, and particularly to his colleagues Messrs. Harold M. Bannerman and C. Ervin Brown for critical reading resulting in the correction of obvious errors and the addition of certain items.

CONTENTS

Preface	v
Introductory	13
Map No. 1	22
The State of Merimak—Map No. 1	23
Mohawk—Map No. 1	25
Chesapeak—Map No. 1	30
Some comments on Map No. 1	34
Map No. 2	36
Cherokee—Map No. 2	37
Map No. 3	40
Ohio—Map No. 3	41
Michigan—Map No. 3	45
Map. No. 4	49
Iowa—Map No. 4	50
Map No. 5	54
Arkansa—Map. No. 5	55
Map No. 6	59
Texas—Map No. 6	60
Map No. 7	63
Dakota—Map No. 7	64
Map No. 8	69

Arizona—Map No. 8   70

Map No. 9   74

Calvada—Map No. 9   75

Oregon—Map No. 9   79

Political, Social and Economic Dividends of Reorganization   82

   1. Representation   82

   2. Law-Enforcement   83

   3. Taxation   84

   4. Industrial Control   85

   5. The Federal Structure   86

Washington, the National Capital   90

Liabilities and Hazards of Reorganization   93

Conclusion   95

Summation   98

Map No. 10   98 - 99

Appendix   101

BACK TO
THIRTEEN STATES

INTRODUCTORY

The United States is, are—take it either way you like—
a mess. Let us confine observations to the forty-eight states
of the continental domain, some three million square miles
containing presently more than 200 million people living
in the most complexly industrialized society the world has
ever known, and attempting to cope with its problems of
overpopulation, pollution, and social maladjustment through
the medium of a political structure created 200 years ago
and constructed to deal specifically with the conditions of
a simple agricultural-commercial age in which the axe, the
horse, the plow and the sailing ship were prime implements
of existence and communication. Would anyone in his right
mind attempt to construct a modern apartment building
with an axe and a hand-saw, or to send an urgent message
from New York to Savannah by horse courier or sailboat?

At the root of many of our difficulties, in the writer's
opinion, is the chaotic architecture of our federal structure
which evolved Topsy-fashion from the thirteen colonies as
a base, and was expanded by political opportunism to en-
compass a large part of the North American continent. The
original thirteen states resulted from one hundred and fifty
years of colonization, mainly British, but involving much
rivalry and occasional wars with or between other European
powers, including France, Spain, the Netherlands, and Swe-
den, as well as almost ceaseless resistance from the numerous Indian tribes that were being dispossessed. The colonies
developed from land grants made by English kings to various ambitious, adventurous or needy members or groups,
chiefly of the English nobility. The geography of the lands
granted in this New World being virtually unknown, the

grants usually were defined in terms of prominent coastal features such as capes or harbors, the latter usually situated at the mouths of rivers. From these limits the grants were extended westward on specified parallels of latitude "from sea to sea." As colonization proceeded, charters were revised, revoked, reduced in size, or even extended. The grantees and their assigns sold and sub-divided again and again, but geographical knowledge usually lagged far behind the developers' ambitions. Therefore, the convenient methods of defining boundaries were in terms of rivers, or of cardinal directions, usually parallels of latitude, less often longitudinal. In one strange case the arc of a circle having a radius of twelve *English statute miles* centered on New Castle, Delaware was specified, and this still prevails as the southeastern corner of Pennsylvania. Rivers, in many cases, were specified "to their farthest source," which was then unknown and later a subject for much disagreement. Just which small spring or rivulet is the proper "source" of a great river? Neighboring grantees tended to interpret the matter to their own advantage, and arguments often ensued.

The result was an incredible snarl of conflicting claims, part of which were settled by compromises in colonial days, but many of which persisted long afterward and resulted in numerous appeals to the Supreme Court of the United States—one between Massachusetts and Rhode Island even appearing there twice.[1] Several of the colonies maintained conflicting claims to territories west of the Appalachians, but these generally were settled by cession to the Federal Government at the time of its establishment or in the next few decades. Incidentally, all settlements of interstate boundary conflicts must be approved by the Congress of the United States.

---

1. For a good review of the status and history of state boundaries, see U.S. Geological Survey Bulletin 1212: *Boundaries of the United States and the Several States,* 1966.

Let us now examine the results of subdivision by rivers or compass bearings. For the early colonists, rivers afforded the easiest natural routes for travel and exploration. Overland, they formed serious barriers to transportation, hence were sensible boundaries. However, as settlement proceeded and industrialization developed, this situation was altered drastically. River valleys still afford useful routes for overland travel and transport in some cases, but their importance is greatly diminished; and as obstacles, rivers are virtually eliminated. In the eastern United States, where rivers are most numerous but drainage basins and states are comparatively small in area, the two sides of a river basin commonly are very similar in topography, climate, flora, fauna and utility as evaluated in human terms. The valley lowlands usually provide the choicest land for agriculture, industry and housing, and river mouths, in many cases, afford natural harbors for foreign and coastal commerce. The populations on either side of a river naturally are apt to be very similar in origin, aims and occupation. Rivers, therefore, constitute the worst possible boundaries for major political subdivisions, since *they split groups of similar people with common goals and problems right down the middle!* The effects are especially deplorable in the case of major ports, such as New York, where the use of waterways as boundaries fragments the nation's greatest shipping center into two major ports, and necessitates the creation of a cumbersome Port Authority. Other less striking examples are Portsmouth, N.H., and Portland, Ore., Boston, Baltimore, New Orleans, San Francisco and Seattle, situated entirely within single states, are fortunate to escape these jurisdictional problems.

Similar dislocations along interior rivers are innumerable. Almost every important river city or town has its minor counterpart on the opposite shore, which is likely to be in another state. Yet the two communities are dependent on the mutual conjunction of industry and commerce, and would prosper best under a common jurisdiction. Examples are Philadelphia, Pa., and Camden, N.J.; Cincinnati, O., and Covington, Ky.; St. Louis, Mo., and East St. Louis, Ill., plus Granite City and several other Illinois communities; Omaha, Neb., and Council Bluffs, Ia.; Portland, Ore., and Vancouver, Wash.; etc. Could it be that the more symmetrical development of Minneapolis and St. Paul, Minn., is at least partly explainable by their position within a single state, even though divided by a major stream?

Directional boundaries likewise divide closely related populations, although the consequences generally are less serious since they less frequently bisect important urban complexes. This does happen occasionally, as with Kansas City (Mo.-Kan.) and the Chicago, Ill.-Gary, Ind., complex. Applied to drainage basins, however, the results are disastrous. Thus the two latitudinal boundaries of Pennsylvania sever the Susquehanna drainage into three blocks—the headwaters in New York, the main portion in Pennsylvania, and the discharge in Maryland. The same process in Tennessee shatters the Tennessee River Valley into seven stately (?) fragments! Hence T.V.A.! Finally, the checkerboard system applied to the Far West likewise parcels the Colorado River basin among seven states, and makes unavoidable the Colorado River Compact, federally supervised, to apportion its indispensable waters.

Obviously, the basis of political subdivision to meet modern conditions should be drainage basins, as was advocated to a limited degree, but vainly, almost a century ago for the western half of the nation by the eminent geologist and explorer, John Wesley Powell.[2] We shall elaborate on this presently. Meanwhile, to complete our review of existing state boundaries, a casual study yields the following pertinent facts. Excluding international boundaries shared with Canada and Mexico, there are slightly more than 14,-000 miles of interstate borders on straight lines, chiefly

---

2. See Powell, J. W., "Institutions for the Arid Lands," *Century Illus. Mag.*, v. 40, pp. 111-116, 1890.

latitude or longitude. Rivers, measured along major courses, not in detail, supply nearly 6000 miles, largely in the East (including the Mississippi River), where they make up 37 per cent of such boundaries as contrasted with the West (only 19%), the overall average being about 28 per cent. Drainage divides total slightly over 800 miles, or a little over 4 per cent—one per cent in the southern Appalachians (Virginia to West Virginia) and three per cent in the northern Rockies (Montana-Idaho). The problem cities and areas are mainly in the tortuous East, considerably less in the square-set West, practically nil on the divides, East or West.

River boundaries are, indeed, even more troublesome and illogical than already indicated. In many of the original grants and deeds, the ownership of the river itself was unspecified; and this problem eventually was settled by most of the states concerned through agreement on the use of the deepest channel, which is, of course, difficult or impossible to mark out and subject to erosional changes.

But in some cases the original grants specified one or the other riverbank. Thus Maryland in 1632 was granted sovereignty over the Potomac River from its source to its discharge into the Chesapeake Bay *to high-water mark on its southern shore!* This proved so unworkable that it was changed to low-water mark some one hundred and fifty years later, but still results in the anomaly that a duly licensed citizen of Virginia cannot sit on his own shore and fish, legally, in the Potomac River. (He may, by application, obtain at no cost a permit to do so.) Again, the State of Virginia, in ceding to the Federal Government in 1784 its title to land north of the Ohio River, reserved ownership of the waters of that river to its northern shore, and this still applies for the 550 miles by which the river now separates Kentucky and West Virginia from states north and west. In rare cases a certain distance from a river was specified. Thus the Massachusetts-New Hampshire boundary for some thirty miles westward from Newburyport is a zig-zag line *three miles north of* the Merrimack River, and the New York-Connecticut line, though straightened, is still approximately *"twenty miles east of the Hudson."*

The inevitable result of the split sovereignty of the states over major rivers has been that the Federal Government, chiefly through the Corps of Engineers and the U.S. Reclamation Service, has assumed responsibility for most aspects of navigation, flood control and water management, not only on bounding rivers, but to a large degree over all inland waters.

It is clear from the foregoing résumé that the existing pattern of state boundaries is not the product of political clairvoyance on the part of the founding fathers nor of any of our ancestors. Hence, it does not deserve perpetuation simply because of the false halos of local state pride and patriotism, nurtured by well-meaning but short-sighted interests, that have grown up around it like ivy covering old stone walls. Actually the results, with respect to industrial or political organization and even the achievement of social justice, in many respects are deplorable. Many states have little or no effective authority over the sources of their water supply, are so small and limited in the variety of their natural resources that they are in themselves not economically viable, and yet they exercise influence out of all proportion to their importance in the seat of a national government on whose beneficence they, and many of their richer neighbors, have come to depend for supplemental handouts to support them in the style to which they have grown accustomed but which they cannot independently sustain. They are children condemned to perpetual juvenility. Law-enforcement is rendered virtually inoperative in many of the most critical areas by the complex intertangle of state boundaries, (e.g. the New York City interstate area, or the Great Lakes shoreline, etc.), and the control of transportation, pollution, public health efforts and orderly development, snarled in the endless red tape of state compacts subject to federal approval, becomes almost impossible.

Consider, for instance, the absurdity of a union of sovereign and theoretically equal states, at least as represented in the United States Senate, or to a lesser degree in the Electoral College, which are as unequal in area and population as the following:

TABLE I

COMPARISONS OF VARIOUS STATES

STATES	RATIOS	
	Area	Population
Texas to Rhode Island	220 to 1	12 to 1
California to Rhode Island	137 to 1	21 to 1
Texas to Nevada	2.4 to 1	23 to 1
California to Nevada	1.4 to 1	41 to 1
New York to Vermont	5.3 to 1	41 to 1
New York to Vermont and New Hampshire	2.5 to 1	15 to 1
Pennsylvania to Montana	0.3 to 1	17 to 1
California to Wyoming	1.6 to 1	60 to 1

The fact that the comparative natural resources of these various states are correspondingly disproportionate, though not necessarily in parallel fashion, scarcely needs documentation, though it would be a simple matter. The New York to Vermont plus New Hampshire ratios are cited because they involve areas that closely resemble each other in climate, topography, and, aside from urban complexes, in population characteristics, and each has very limited access to the sea. They thus emphasize the disparity now existing between inherently similar regions, even when directly connected one to the other, as is not the case in most of the situations cited.

It is proposed here to suggest for public discussion a regrouping of the areas of the continental United States that would afford for the present, and for a reasonable guesstimate of the near but unforeseeable future, a considerable degree of equality and sovereign viability. Perhaps for reasons of sentimentality, though there is nothing sacred about the number, a concentration into thirteen superstates is projected as a workable combination. Where possible, the names of key states are retained for the proposed superstates, provided these are of native, generally Indian, origin; and where this has not seemed feasible, others that seem appropriate, preferably, though not always, of similar origin, are suggested.

Again, there is nothing sacred about these names. However, it is urged that this nation has outlived the usefulness and propriety of such colonial nomenclatures as New Hampshire, Georgia, and even Mary Land. Let us cast off the last vestiges of empire subservience, and shed any nostalgic patriotism for such darling phrases as "Dear Old Virginny," or "Little Rhodie." Consign them, if you must, to roles of purely local, not national, significance.

It seems obvious that the geography of climate and water supply should be the overriding consideration in a sensible revision of state boundaries. Our whole agricultural-industrial-social complex, with its resultant environmental problems of pollution and waste, is conditioned by the available water supply and its utilization more than by any other set of factors, and this lends itself readily to subdivision into compact regions of unique character that require special treatment. Specifically, the regions should be drainage basins, either singly or in groups of similar character, as far as possible complete. However, the great size of the central

Mississippi River basin, with its wide diversity of climate, necessitates some carefully tailored subdivision. For a beginning, let us start, as the colonists did, on the East Coast, with New England.

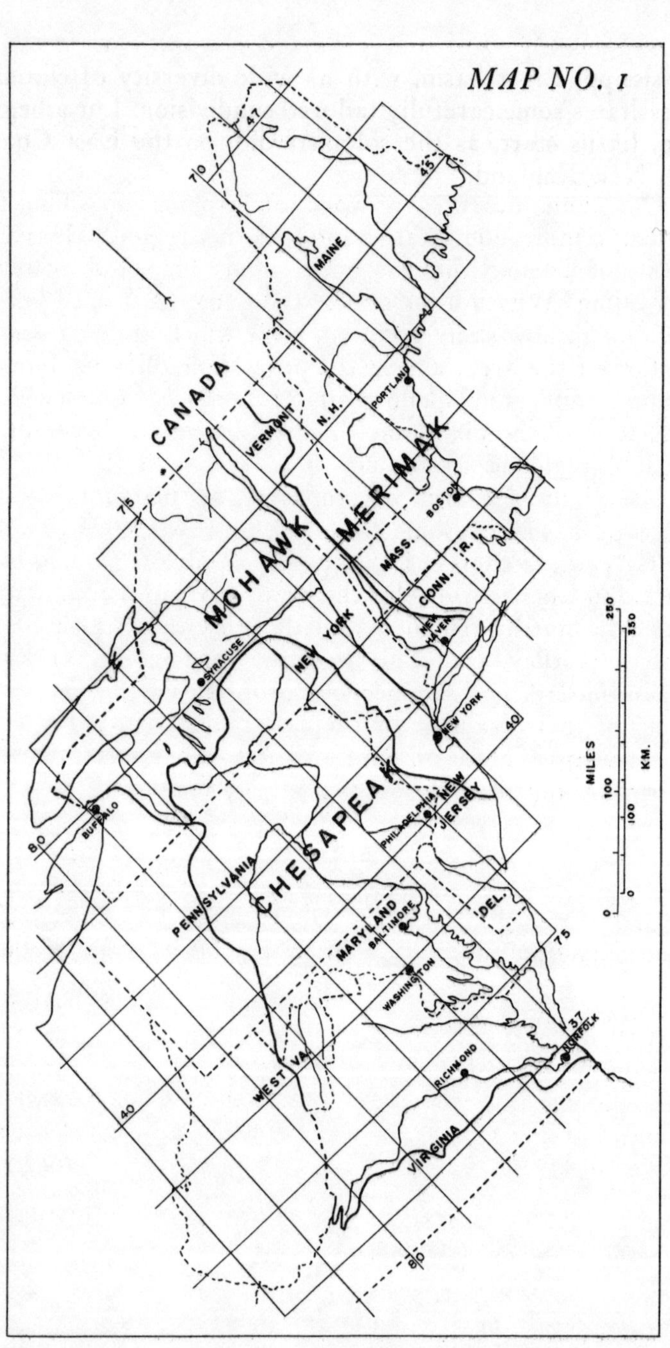

MAP NO. 1
CANADA
MAINE
VERMONT
N. H.
MASS.
CONN.
R. I.
NEW YORK
NEW HAVEN
BOSTON
PORTLAND
MOHAWK
MERIMAK
CHESAPEAK
SYRACUSE
BUFFALO
NEW YORK
PHILADELPHIA
NEW JERSEY
DEL.
PENNSYLVANIA
MARYLAND
BALTIMORE
WASHINGTON
WEST VA.
RICHMOND
NORFOLK
VIRGINIA
47
45
70
75
80
40
37
75
40
80
MILES
KM.
250
350
100
100
0
0

THE STATE OF MERIMAK—MAP NO. 1

The name deserves a word of explanation. The two authentic indigenous state names of this region, Massachusetts and Connecticut, are both unduly long and awkward in spelling. Why not substitute the name of a once beautiful, though now sadly polluted, river which drains a central portion of the area, and in the process simplify its unnecessarily complicated spelling of *Merrimack*? Otherwise, a reduction of existing state names either to Masacut or Conicut might be acceptable.

Essentially this area encompasses, in their entirety, the drainage basins of some half-dozen fair-sized rivers, particularly the Penobscot, Kennebec, Androscoggin, Merrimack and Connecticut, plus the headwaters of a few streams that flow northward into Canada and which must be accepted as they are. The western portions of Vermont, Massachusetts and Connecticut properly belong, by virtue either of their drainage or their propinquity, to New York. The proposed State of Merimak, therefore, comprises the following approximate areas and populations.

TABLE II

MERIMAK

Contributing States	Area—Sq. Mi.	Population
Maine*	32,215	993,663
New Hampshire*	9,304	737,681
Vermont	3,840	138,092
Massachusetts	7,400	5,539,768
Connecticut	3,000	1,369,455
Rhode Island*	1,214	949,723
Total	56,973	9,728,382

* Entire. All others subdivided.

Admittedly this region lacks many of the natural resources on which the grimy industrialization of other areas has been established. It has no important metal mines, no workable coal, no oil or gas, nor any likelihood of their discovery unless it might be under its coastal waters—which God forbid! It has perhaps the least proportion of tillable land in the eastern half of the country, but, conversely, more forest area, which eases the problems of flood control and adds immeasurably to the scenic and recreational values, which are high. It has substantial resources in water power and is excessively endowed with an abundance of shoreline of much natural beauty and practical value. With these advantages offsetting its liabilities, and with the aid of its traditional Yankee ingenuity, it should constitute a highly viable and enviously attractive unit in a modern series of thirteen sovereign states. As reconstituted, it could completely control the distribution and police the quality of its plentiful water supply, and protect its invaluable coastal waters from ruinous pollution, without the necessity of endless federally promoted or supervised state compacts. Its resources would be adequate to support competent departments of surface transportation, forestry, geological or mineral resource bureaus, agencies of tourism, departments of fishery and marine life, and many other aspects necessary to effective organization, which, for the most part, are poorly serviced or not at all in much of the inadequate existing state governmental machinery. And all without the necessity of any lost motion and overhead costs through federal intervention or participation.

Statistically, Merimak would rank as the twelfth of thirteen states in area, the 11th in population, but, owing to the large number of important urban centers, the fourth in average density of population—even though it probably encompasses a larger percentage of relatively thinly populated forested land than any other proposed regional area.

Thanks to its lack of mineral resources, Merimak would

have less than average difficulty coping with its nonetheless urgent pollution problems, deriving mainly from its pulp and wood products industries, its textile factories, and its light-manufacturing plants. It fortunately escapes the massive problems of the coal-and-oil-producing states, with their heavy industries and refineries.

Climatically, it is blessed with a fairly adequate rainfall in the range of 30 inches per annum, reasonably evenly distributed, and conducive, along with its superb shoreline, to the development of exceptional tourist and travel attraction not only in summer but even, in numerous localities, also in winter.

MOHAWK—MAP NO. 1

Next comes perhaps our most difficult problem, but one of the most critical: how to reconstitute New York. Politically, the most urgent reform facing the nation with respect to local self-government, it seems to me, is to bring Metropolitan New York, including adjacent areas of New Jersey and Connecticut, under one unified authority, and to give the superstate control over enough shoreline to make its problems of pollution and waste disposal as nearly manageable as is humanly possible. To accomplish this, it seems essential to include substantially all the shore facing Long Island, and also the northern half of New Jersey down almost to Atlantic City. New Haven may feel some pangs at separation from New England, but actually it is in effect inexorably becoming more and more a satellite of New York City.

In addition to being thus expanded at the south, to include all drainages between the Delaware Basin on the west and the Connecticut River on the east, the new state likewise should include the westward drainage of the Green Mountains tributary to the Champlain Valley. The fertile and highly industrialized Mohawk Valley, with its extension in the Finger Lakes area draining into Lake Ontario, as well as the minor drainage systems flowing northward out of the Adirondacks into Canada, logically belongs with the New York metropolitan complex—however much the inhabitants of these areas sometimes regret this condition of their existence. They can hardly do without the New York City market for their products and its magnificent outlet for their integrated transportation complex. Nor can New York City exist without its sustaining hinterland and the safety valve it provides for escape and recreation. Along with this, of course, should go a realignment of the greater New York City urban area under some sort of effective metropolitan government, to include all the compact city complex in adjacent Long Island and New Jersey. But that is another story.

The fantastic suggestion sometimes advanced in sheer frustration that New York City secede from New York State illustrates the extent of the irritations existing in present circumstances. It is not contended that the realignment of state limits as here proposed would cure this condition, though it should ease it a little. To divorce the city from its countryside would deprive it of all control, or even influence, over its lifelines of water and food supply and would lead to open warfare in place of the present political rivalry. City and country, the nation over, must simply adjust to their matrimonial necessities.

Looking westward, it seems essential to separate two relatively minor areas from the present limits of New York State. First, on the far west, is that territory draining into Lake Erie and including the city of Buffalo. The reasons will be clearer when we approach the problems of the Great Lakes as a whole, even though we are here permitting Mohawk to retain its interest in Lake Ontario. Obviously, the superstate must include that portion of the international (Canadian) boundary extending from the Green Mountains westward to and along the St. Lawrence River. Moreover, the Mohawk Valley-Syracuse-Rochester-Niagara Falls region is probably considerably more closely linked industrially with New York City and the Hudson Valley than with Midwestern patterns of exploitation in the Great Lakes area. Also, the problems of pollution in the Great Lakes are already rather fully developed by the time their waters reach Lake Ontario, so that this stretch may as well be left as it is.

The second problem area is that of the headwaters of the Delaware and Susquehanna rivers, which originate in the westward- and southward-draining slopes of the Catskill upland. These properly belong with the problems of the Chesapeake and Delaware bays, as we shall see presently. Admittedly, since New York City now obtains its chief water supply through diversion tunnels from the headwaters of the Delaware (by the grace of compacts with the states of Pennsylvania and New Jersey) it may be necessary to accept this situation as a "fait accompli" and permit Mohawk to retain this area, which is neither unduly large nor very populous. However, for purposes of this discussion, it and the upper Susquehanna Basin are excluded. Superficially it might appear that the state's major stream, the Hudson River, logically should be its chief source of water supply. Although the possibility of using lower Hudson water often has been raised for discussion, it has never seemed feasible because the main portion of the Hudson for 150 miles above New York City practically to Albany is tidal and more or less saline, in addition to its excess of modern pollution. Complete chemical renovation would be required to render it usable. Moreover, the fresh water supplied by the Hudson sources in the Adirondacks and the limited Mohawk Valley drainage from westward is scarcely more than adequate to cover local needs of the numerous sizable cities and minor industrial towns of that area, especially as they may be expected to grow in the future. Lake Champlain might conceivably be tapped to supplement New York City supplies to some degree, but with Canada's interests involved this solution likewise has limitations.

The approximate area and population of the proposed new entity of Mohawk would be as follows:

TABLE III

MOHAWK

Contributing States	Area—Sq. Mi.	Population
New York	39,576	16,060,794
Connecticut	2,009	1,662,762
New Jersey	2,600	4,961,278
Massachusetts	857	149,402
Vermont	5,769	306,640
Total	50,811	23,140,876

This revision gives the new superstate an area of 50,811 square miles, smallest in our entire thirteen, but a population of over 23 millions, ranking it third in the nation as to total, but still with nearly twice the average density per square mile (455) of its nearest competitors, Michigan and Chesapeak (regrouped). This rearrangement would place the new state in complete control of its natural sources of water supply, the Hudson-Mohawk river system plus the Lake Champlain Basin and the Housatonic Valley, as well as of numerous minor streams draining northward into Lake Ontario and the St. Lawrence. It would provide it with enough ocean shoreline to cope with its shipping industry, its waste disposal, and its recreational problems on a regional basis—and even, if desirable, with the possible conversion of Long Island Sound into a fresh-water (?) lake, as has been seriously proposed.

Its resources would remain essentially the same as those of the present state of New York, comprising a valuable agricultural belt lengthwise along the Hudson-Mohawk Valley and westward south of Lake Ontario, flanked by substantial forest and recreational areas in the bordering mountains; and embracing in the Adirondacks an exceptional reserve of great natural and recreational value, well watered, largely forested, and with large portions under state ownership. Substantial resources of iron ore, zinc, titanium, talc, etc. are exploited in the Adirondacks; large reserves of salt are developed in the western portions of the state, along with minor production of oil and gas, some of which, however, would be lost in the proposed realignment of boundaries. Altogether these resources, coupled with its incomparable port facilities for ocean shipping, vastly improved by unification, should make it a much more viable entity both economically and politically.

A word perhaps about the name "MOHAWK." As with Merimak, this, the name of a minor but central and vital stream, derived from Indian background, seems generally most appropriate. Surely *New* York is no longer new, and what was York anyway?

Hudson is, indeed, the major stream, but why should we elevate a mercenary Dutch voyager to such a pinnacle? Manhatan, thus simplified in spelling, might be appropriate for the city; but let us not incite rebellion by inflicting it on the up-staters, who will insist on being unhappy in any case at the prospect of enlarging their state on the ocean-front and diminishing it in some of their favorite fishing and hunting territory. For the loss of Buffalo and the problems of Lake Erie, all probably will feel relief as long as Niagara is still theirs.

Consideration was given to the possibility of including the entire Delaware Basin, and the Philadelphia-Wilmington urban complex in the Mohawk grouping. This would tend to equalize superstate areas somewhat and would simplify water supply problems on the Upper Delaware Valley slightly. However, the water supply, transportation and pollution problems of the Delaware and Chesapeake bays are so intimately intertwined that this disposition would create even greater complications; and, furthermore, it would greatly unbalance the distribution of populations.

CHESAPEAK—MAP NO. 1

Chesapeak (why add the useless "e?") comprises all areas tributary to the Delaware and Chesapeake bays, the principal rivers being the Delaware, Susquehanna, Potomac and James. Its population is concentrated axially along the urban complex stretching from Philadelphia through Wilmington, Baltimore and Washington to Richmond. Seven existing states and the District of Columbia are involved, as shown in the following table.

TABLE IV
CHESAPEAK

Contributing States	Area—Sq. Mi.	Population
New York	7,000	767,484
Pennsylvania	30,333	8,024,899
New Jersey	5,236	2,206,886
Delaware*	2,057	548,104
Maryland	10,077	3,912,399
West Virginia	3,500	125,495
Virginia	27,315	3,811,449
District of Columbia*	70	756,510
Total	85,588	20,153,226

* Entire. All others subdivided.

Thus constituted it ranks eleventh in area, fifth in population, and third, but close to second, in average density of population—well over 200 per square mile.

The overriding reason for combining fragments from so many existing political units is the absolute necessity of obtaining centralized, effective control over the inland waters of the Chesapeake and Delaware bays, which, next to the Great Lakes, constitute the largest, most valuable aquatic resource within the continental boundary, and one which is most immediately threatened with fatal pollution. The two bays must be treated as a unit because they now are connected by a navigation canal that is in the process of being deepened and enlarged to accommodate major ocean shipping, and which threatens to divert much of the surplus fresh water that now precariously preserves the viability of aquatic life in the Chesapeake waters into the waters of the Delaware Bay, which already are, for practical purposes, dead.

The absurdity of the present political boundaries is obvious from the map. The Delaware River system, originating in New York, for much of its course forms the boundary between Pennsylvania and New Jersey, but just before discharging into the bay becomes the boundary between New Jersey and Delaware. The result is classic: New York City gets the pure water from the headwaters, Pennsylvania and New Jersey divide the still-useful lower flow however they can agree. Poor, helpless Delaware, too small to count for much anyway, gets the sewage.

The Susquehanna rises in the lovely rural countryside of southern New York State, but just before debouching into Pennsylvania receives the waste and pollution of the large Binghamton industrial area—a good riddance for New York but unfortunate for Pennsylvania, which immediately compounds this by adding the acid waters of the world's largest anthracite coal-mine complex and speeds it onward to mix with Harrisburg's sewage, joyfully delivering the resulting mess to Maryland just 20 miles above its entry into Chesapeake Bay.

The Potomac Basin is equally atrociously subdivided, thanks particularly to the incredible jigsaw-puzzle boundaries of Western Maryland and eastern West Virginia. Even a small area in Pennsylvania is involved. For the rest, the lower Potomac separates Maryland and Virginia.

So it is that in order to deal with any overall problem involving the Delaware Basin, four states must agree to a compact, which generally must be, or ends by being, controlled basically by the Federal Government. The Susquehanna involves three states, dropping two of the Delaware group but adding one. For the Potomac, four states, two of them new to the previous combinations, are concerned; and here the Federal Government, through the District of Columbia, assumes a dominant role. Only the James River in southern Virginia lies wholly within one existing state. How much simplification, with at least the means for genuine improvement, might be attained by combining this whole area into a single unit! Admittedly, internal state politics would still continue; but the necessity of multiplying this four times over to achieve any major or even minor objective would disappear.

Economically, the superstate of Chesapeak would have a much broader and sounder base than any of its existing contributors and a much better unified community of interests. Its economy would include a fairly important agricultural base, a considerable mineral production, mainly of coal, but additionally important in iron ore and zinc with other possibilities. In ocean commerce and its resultant activities, it would contend more evenly with the New York area; and, provided it could solve the problem of preserving the Chespeake and restoring the Delaware Bay, it could maintain its predominant place in the inland fisheries industries which are now so seriously endangered. Such unification also would facilitate greatly the urgently needed establishment of a unified transport system in the highly urbanized corridor from Philadelphia to Richmond, and would remove the legal barriers that now so greatly hamper police control across the state lines.

As indicated in Table IV, it is assumed that simple logic and justice would require the inclusion of the District of Columbia in the new superstate, with the opportunity of enjoying the benefits of local self-government—as is now taking place partially, willy-nilly, by the endless expansion of U.S. Government activities beyond the District's limits.

As in New England—pardon me, Merimak—the new state would be able to support far more effective and better unified state services, such as police, transport control, public health, natural resources. Only Pennsylvania and possibly Maryland have reasonably adequate mineral-resource controls at present.

As for a name, Chesapeak seems to me the best suggestion, since the great bay is the outstanding feature of the region. Supposedly the name is of authentic Indian origin, although what it signified seems to be mostly conjecture. An acceptable alternative might be Potomac. Surely Wm. Penn, the Virgin Queen, and Mary deserve to be relegated to the attic along with Lord Delaware and *New* Jersey, which now hardly bears the bloom of youth.

The three superstates represented on this map cover a total of 193,372 square miles, a smaller area than that of any but one of the proposed remaining ten. However, these three contained over fifty-three million people in 1970, just slightly more than one-fourth of the population of the continental United States. The average density per square mile was 274, and thus more than four times the average for the country as a whole—eight times that west of the Mississippi. This situation exists in spite of the fact that the region, in general, possesses a much-higher-than-average proportion of well-forested, moderately rugged land, which is but thinly inhabited and ideal for vacation land, summer or winter. This extends from the mountains of Maine, New Hampshire and Vermont into Massachusetts and western Connecticut, resuming in the Hudson highlands to continue along the Appalachian ridges through Pennsylvania into Virginia and beyond. Add to this the western outposts of the Adirondacks, plus the Catskills, the Poconos and the Allegheny front, and one must marvel at the natural endowments of this still-lovely although sadly scarred natural paradise.

This fortunate situation is created by the combination of a temperate, though rather unequable, climate blessed with an adequate supply of rainfall ranging from about 30 inches in the far north to 40 or more southward, and reasonably distributed throughout the year. Since the percentage of level, tillable land is rather low in most of the region, agriculture is of only minor importance and mainly for specialized crops. Moreover, the ever-increasing pressure of urban and industrial development tends to pre-empt much of the better agricultural area that does exist.

Although mineral resources are of importance in a few categories, they, like agriculture, are of only minor significance. The real life-blood of the economy is supplied by its tremendous volume of commerce, especially overseas, by the quantity and diversity of its manufactures, and especially by the concentration into New York, plus Boston, Philadelphia, etc., of the financial control of enterprises not only within but far beyond the immediate borders of this region. Coupled to this is the similar concentration of federal governmental machinery and operations in Washington, and, by uncontrollable expansion, far beyond but mainly along the Washington-New York axis. These conditions are, of course, partly the result of history. The nation celebrates Philadelphia, 1776, as its birthplace. The relative importance of the region, naturally, probably will tend to diminish somewhat in the future as it has in the past, but its absolute size is likely to continue its seemingly inexorable pattern of growth.

Thanks to the climatic factors and cultural patterns just enumerated, the supply of water up to the present time has been more than ample and its quality by nature excellent. Unfortunately this condition is rapidly reaching the point of reversal. All larger streams and most of the larger inland waters are already either very badly polluted or seriously threatened, and the actual suppply of water for many cities and industries is approaching or has exceeded the limits of adequacy and demands supplementary sources or rationing, with rigid controls to assure the maintenance of quality. Surely these conditions are not likely to be met by the continued dispersal of control among 14 separate states, or the existing subdivision of countless drainage units among several of the fourteen entities, the whole umpired by endless layers of federal bureaucracy in Washington.

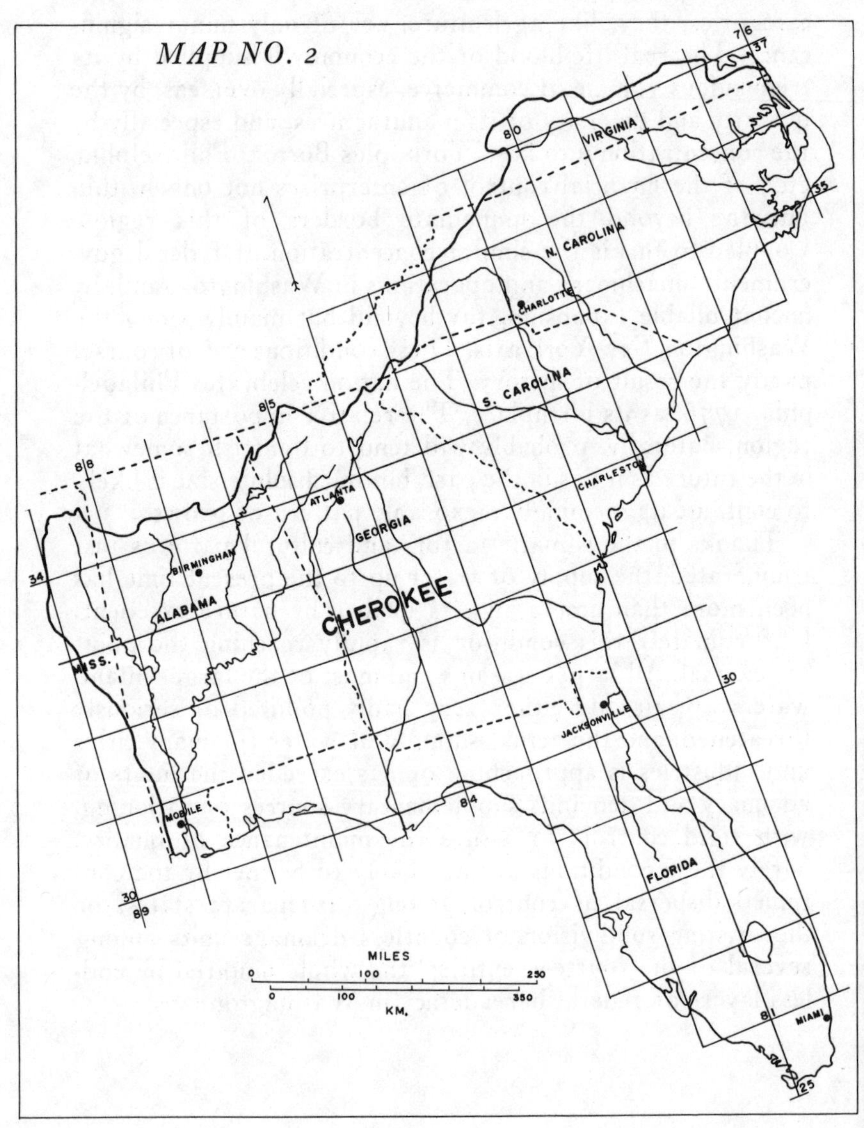

MAP NO. 2
76
37
80
VIRGINIA
35
N. CAROLINA
CHARLOTTE
S. CAROLINA
85
88
CHARLESTON
ATLANTA
GEORGIA
34
BIRMINGHAM
ALABAMA
CHEROKEE
MISS.
30
JACKSONVILLE
84
MOBILE
FLORIDA
30
89
MILES
0
100
250
0
100
350
KM.
81
MIAMI
25

CHEROKEE—MAP NO. 2

We now can breathe a little easier in the wider open spaces. The proposed superstate of CHEROKEE, honoring a proud and sadly mistreated Indian confederation which originally occupied its Appalachian axis and eastward seaboard, is constructed as follows:

TABLE V
CHEROKEE

Contributing States	Area—Sq. Mi.	Population
Virginia	6,000	424,529
North Carolina	45,712	4,653,619
South Carolina*	31,055	2,590,516
Georgia	57,676	4,501,661
Florida*	58,560	6,789,443
Alabama	42,169	3,070,441
Mississippi	5,500	172,470
Total	246,672	22,202,679

* Entire. All others subdivided.

Two states, South Carolina and Florida, are taken in their entirety, three others are very largely included, two (Virginia and Mississippi) contribute minor areas, and a relatively insignificant fraction from Tennessee has been ignored. The summation comes to almost a quarter of a million square miles, or nearly one-twelfth of the continental area, with more than 22 million inhabitants. The rank is eighth in area and fourth in population, with an average density of 81 per square mile—generally considerably more evenly distributed than in the northeast, with much less concentration into urban complexes. This condition reflects the much higher proportion of reasonably level terrain with deep soil and the far greater percentage of agricultural land. Nevertheless, owing to the poorly drained nature of much of the large area of coastal plain on the one hand, and the considerable amount of rugged mountainous land along the Appalachian divide, there are still large stands of forest, albeit badly mutilated in most places by repeated careless cutting—as is true of course nearly everywhere in the eastern United States, but particularly in the Appalachians.

Once the land of cotton for nearly a century, and with its soil sadly depleted and wasted in the process, this region is still strongly based on agriculture, but of a much more diversified nature. It specializes particularly in tobacco and in fruits and vegetables, with dairying for local needs, etc. Forest products are quite important, and manufacturing, especially of tobacco products, chemicals, textiles and fertilizers, has grown rapidly in recent decades. Iron ore and coal are important locally around Birmingham, Ala.; phosphate production is large in Florida and is developing rapidly in the Carolinas; and miscellaneous minor products (clay, barite, lithium) are mined in the Appalachians. Florida cultivates the gold of sunshine, tourism and land-development with spectacular success.

The region is favored with a much milder climate than the northeast, a longer growing season, and considerably more rainfall (45 to 55 inches per annum generally), fairly well distributed. The increasing violence and intensity of storms southward, however, brings problems of flood control, swamp drainage, oceanfront damage and shoreline changes which have invited much attention from the U.S. Corps of Engineers, always busy with new ditches or dams, and shore preservation or improvement.

The drainage pattern consists of numerous small rivers which originate in the Appalachians and flow radially southeast and south either into the Atlantic or the Gulf, except in Florida, where drainage is local and chaotic. These numerous systems, many of them having considerable similarity, would be well suited for unification under centralized control, rather than, as now, having several of them either serve as boundary lines between states, or cross state boundaries, in either case dispersing control and responsibility.

The proposed superstate would have bright prospects of becoming a national leader speaking with a powerful voice. Its many small and frequently inadequate state services, such as highway and transportation departments, health and welfare offices, forest and agricultural services, mineral resource bureaus, etc. could function on a scale that should be far more efficient. The state could readily assume full responsibility for all the public works programs now ceded to the Federal Government.

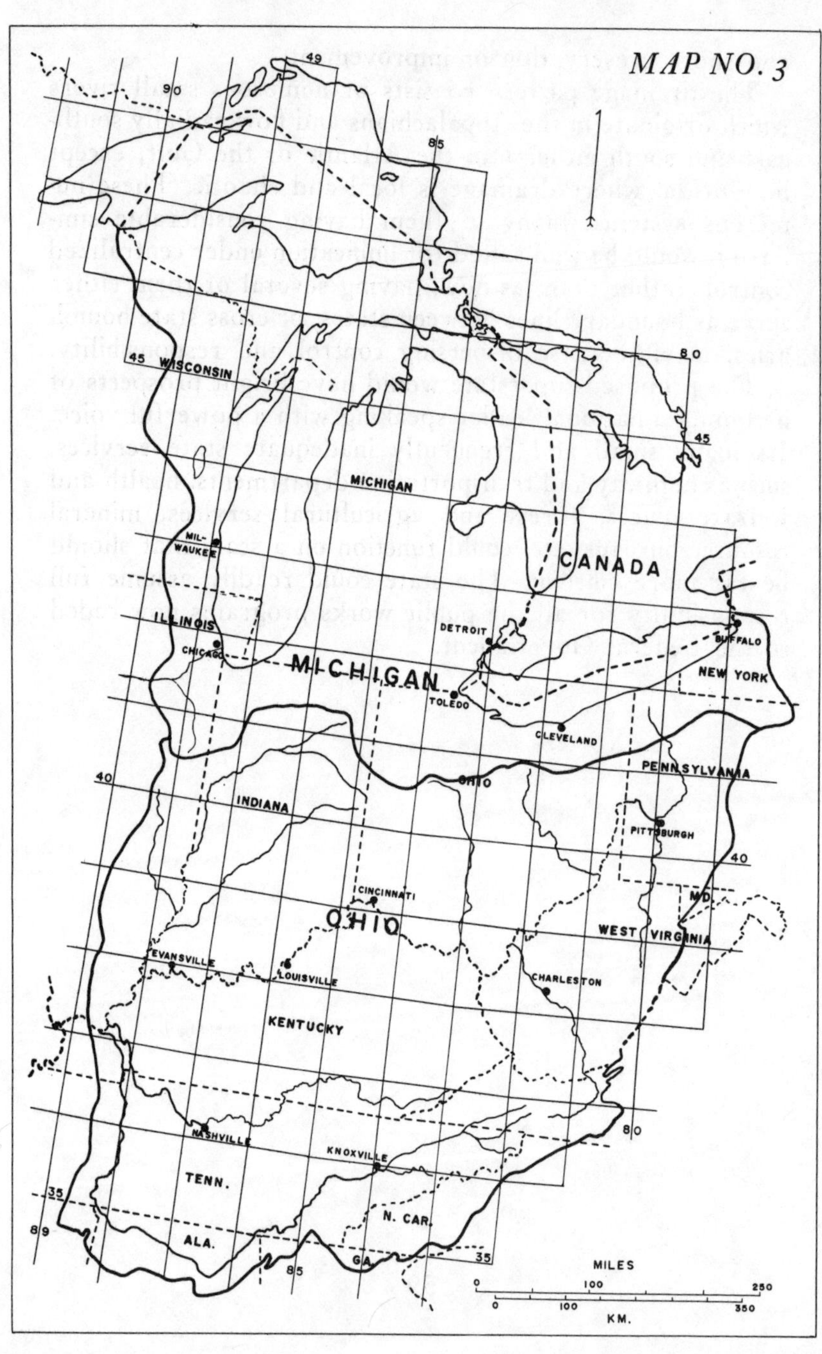

MAP NO. 3
49
90
85
80
WISCONSIN
45
MICHIGAN
MIL-
WAUKEE
CANADA
45
ILLINOIS
MICHIGAN
DETROIT
BUFFALO
CHICAGO
NEW YORK
TOLEDO
CLEVELAND
PENNSYLVANIA
40
OHIO
INDIANA
PITTSBURGH
CINCINNATI
40
OHIO
MD.
WEST VIRGINIA
EVANSVILLE
LOUISVILLE
CHARLESTON
KENTUCKY
80
NASHVILLE
KNOXVILLE
TENN.
35
N. CAR.
89
ALA.
GA.
85
35
MILES
0   100   250
0   100   350
KM.

OHIO—MAP NO. 3

This proposed superstate, retaining appropriately the name of its principal and central river and of one of its most important constituent parts, is constructed as follows:

TABLE VI
OHIO

Contributing States	Area—Sq. Mi.	Population
Maryland	500	10,000
West Virginia	20,580	1,618,742
Virginia	7,500	412,516
North Carolina	7,000	428,440
Georgia	1,200	87,914
Alabama	10,000	373,724
Mississippi	1,000	47,119
Tennessee	33,744	2,817,401
Kentucky	39,395	3,166,571
Pennsylvania	13,500	3,424,014
Ohio	31,222	6,505,779
Indiana	28,791	3,954,640
Illinois	9,500	514,961
Total	203,932	23,361,821

The entire Ohio River drainage, with very minor exceptions, is involved, including the basins of its two virtually independent tributaries, the Cumberland and Tennessee rivers, which debouche into the Ohio so near its mouth and confluence with the Mississippi that they actually constitute separate drainage systems. Its area of over 200,000 square miles ranks ninth in our grouping, but its population of more than twenty-three million gives it second rank. The average density, over 100 per square mile, is fifth and reflects a fairly widespread and even distribution rather than an excessive concentration into great urban complexes, as was typical for Map No. 1, the Northeastern trio. There are, it is true, a number of sizable cities, particularly Pittsburgh and Cincinnati. No state is wholly included within the proposed boundaries, although the greater part of five states is covered, plus an important portion of Pennsylvania and minor edges of seven others—thirteen contributors in all.

The eastern third of this region is fairly rugged, falling either in the Appalachian system of ridges and valleys on the south or the deeply dissected Allegheny plateau to the north. The remainder, however, is comparatively flat, especially north of the Ohio River, and constitutes heartland agricultural territory. The average rainfall ranges generally from near 40 inches annually in the north and west to 50 or more in the south and east, and is favorably distributed for agricultural purposes, but often concentrated into storms or cycles conducive to extensive flooding, especially in the southeast.

The area is intensively developed both agriculturally and industrially, the industrial output tending, perhaps, to gradually exceed the value of agricultural products, but without great disparity. Mineral output is quite important. The principal bituminous coal region of the nation is centered in West Virginia and western Pennsylvania, with extensions into eastern Kentucky and Tennessee and some reappearance in western Kentucky, Illinois, etc. Oil and gas are produced in considerable volume. Important zinc deposits plus some iron, copper, fluorite, and phosphate are exploited. The steel industry, based on imported iron ore and local coal, is concentrated around Pittsburgh, along with many satellite metallurgical and manufacturing industries. Agriculturally, corn and soybeans are staples, and locally tobacco.

Livestock also is very important, especially hogs and cattle, but also horses, sheep, etc. in various localities. Altogether, it is a great country, but—.

The result of all this activity, especially the industrial output, but aided and abetted by agriculture, is pollution on a colossal scale. Even as long ago as 1936, the date of one of the most comprehensive nationwide studies of drainage basins and their problems,[1] it was summarized thus: "The Ohio River is a highway, a sewer and a water supply."

Acid mine water entering the streams above Pittsburgh prevented the putrefaction of sewage, delaying its ultimate decay, and additional acid water from steel mills and other plants in the Pittsburgh area intensified the problem. Around Youngstown, it was reported that "Concentrated use and reuse of polluted water by industry" was common, and "sanitary conditions were deplorable."

At Charleston, West Va., "The complex chemical wastes of industries there are not generally susceptible to ordinary treatment methods. . . ."

The problems of the small northern tributaries of the Ohio in that state and in Indiana were listed as especially acute.

The Cumberland and Tennessee valleys at that time suffered similarly though less acutely, but have been industrialized to a much greater degree since.

Doubtless, some progress has been made since 1936 in improving local situations with respect to pollution, particularly in the installation of sewage plants where absent and their improvement elsewhere. But it is exceedingly doubt-

---

1. "Drainage Basin Problems and Programs," National Resources Commission, Govt. Printing Office, 1937.

ful that these measures have been sufficient to counter the enormous increase in the sources of pollutants from intensified industrialization, rapidly increasing population, and the dramatic increase in the use of agricultural pesticides. Numerous excursions through this region by the writer during this particular span of time have afforded no obvious evidence of significant improvement. Quite the contrary!

Some consideration was given to segregating the Tennessee and Cumberland valleys into a separate state, or a different combination with some more southerly territory, but inasmuch as these two rivers debouche into the Ohio they inevitably share substantial areas of mutual interest in control, utilization and navigation. Hence, union with the Ohio Valley proper seems most logical. The combined Tennessee-Cumberland drainage constitutes approximately one-fourth the total area, with a proportionate share of the population. It poses probably the most serious problems of flood control in the area, although the upper Ohio also has suffered acutely on occasion.

Precisely because state control over the region is so thoroughly dispersed among a dozen states, with the Ohio River providing the boundary between portions of six of the more important components, the Federal Government has become involved to an exceptional degree in the establishment and supervision of interstate programs of flood control, power generation, and navigation; and it is likely to be forced to become the chief arbiter and instigator of pollution control under existing circumstances. Under the proposed unification, all these problems *could* be turned over almost completely to local control and administration, with only a modicum of supervision to insure conformity to national objectives. The resulting superstate should rest on one of the soundest foundations in the country, with an opportunity to lead the way in handling the problems of modern society.

We now attempt a rationalization of one of the most urgent and frightening problems of maladjustment in the whole present structure of our crazy-quilt complex of state governments, namely, how to deal with the utilization and avoid the utter ruination of the Great Lakes, until recently the most magnificent series of fresh-water reservoirs on earth. The lower-most lake, Ontario, has already been assigned to the new superstate of Mohawk (essentially New York remodeled for reasons previously stated) except, of course, that roughly one half of it, as with three of the four remaining lakes, belongs to Canada. Since the present state of Michigan is located centrally and is wholly included, in addition to controlling at least 50 percent of the shoreline in question, it seems logical that this good Indian name should be retained for our proposed superstate.

As shown on Map No. 3, seven states are involved (actually eight, but we have excluded Minnesota for reasons to be explained hereafter). The areas and populations contributed by each are listed in Table VII. (*See page 46*)

The proposed superstate ranks 10th in area (101,216 square miles, for the most part exclusive of the Great Lakes themselves, which cover approximately 95,000 square miles) but first in population, with practically 25 million people—one-eighth of the entire country. Most of its area, with the exception of the northern peninsula of Michigan, originally was fertile forest land, first cleared for agriculture and, where not now pre-empted by housing and industrial developments, still agriculturally productive, mainly in the Lower Michigan peninsula. The region likewise contains some valuable mineral resources including salt beds (exploited by underground solution processes) and, in the northern Michi-

TABLE VII
MICHIGAN

Contributing States	Area—Sq. Mi.	Population
New York	3,000	1,362,462
Pennsylvania	1,500	349,996
Ohio	10,000	4,146,238
Indiana	7,500	1,239,029
Illinois	7,000	7,259,732
Michigan*	58,216	8,875,083
Wisconsin	14,000	1,731,000
Total	101,216	24,958,540

* Entire. All others subdivided.

gan peninsula, valuable copper deposits that have been of much importance for more than a century, as well as major iron deposits on which much of the Midwestern industrial complex of steel and coal was developed, thanks to the benefit of cheap lake transportation. These deposits now are of waning importance, but the complex of industries they spawned remains, supplied by other though more remote sources now made available by the Seaway-St. Lawrence water route. There is also, in the southern lake shore area, some minor oil and gas production. With six major industrial cities from Buffalo through Cleveland, Detroit and Chicago to Milwaukee all feeding sewage and factory wastes into these once virginal lake waters, which are said to require centuries (the figure varies widely for individual lakes, being greatest for Lake Superior) for natural renovation, it is no wonder that the last 50 years of human history have been sufficient to render Lake Erie "dead,"

devoid of oxygen to support aquatic life; Lake Ontario
dying; Lake Michigan not far behind, reporting massive
fish kills; and Huron and Superior obviously facing the same
desolation in the none-too-distant future.

Now consider the complexity of the governmental machinery involved in achieving any unified control of this situation. Five states, Wisconsin, Illinois, Indiana, Michigan
and Ohio, are deeply involved, and to a lesser degree also
Pennsylvania and New York. This still omits Minnesota.
To deal with Lake Erie alone, the most vulnerable unit,
requires the cooperation of four major states. No wonder
it is the first to have succumbed! How can any controls be
effective where obstructors can play off five or six or seven
states against each other, then appeal to the Federal Government, and finally arrive at the necessity of accommodation
with the foreign administrations of both Ontario and Canada? Surely this frustrating situation could be simplified
a great deal if it were consolidated for the most part into
the hands of one state organization cooperating with the
federal governments concerned.

Basically, the problem is that, although the lakes originally constituted an enormous reservoir of marvelously
pure water, they are sustained by a relatively meagre annual
replenishment. In addition to the slightly more than 100
thousand square miles of the proposed superstate, plus perhaps 15,000 more at the western end of Lake Superior not
here included, and some 10,000 additional tributary to Lake
Ontario in New York, the entire land drainage from the
United States is only about 120,000 square miles. Allow
a somewhat similar area in Canada, plus the surface of the
lakes themselves and the total is only around 300,000 square
miles. This is in a region having an average rainfall barely
above thirty inches, with only a fractional run-off support-
ing no really major inflowing streams. Add to the 30 million
or so people occupying this basin within the United States
the five or more millions of Canadians on the opposite
shores, and it seems inevitable that at present rates of con-

tamination the lakes must soon become open cesspools, and the St. Lawrence River a gigantic sewer.

In the face of this stark outlook, we have contrived what seems the most promising approach to substituting a workable degree of orderliness in this quagmire of confusion. The actual surface drainage toward the lakes from the south is very narrow, considerably less than 50 miles in width at several places. Since it seems essential that any unit state should control sufficient space to accommodate surface communication (roads, railways, airports) the headwaters of certain southward-flowing streams, particularly in the Chicago area, have been amputated and assigned to Michigan. This would include the area of the always controversial Chicago diversion canal which now connects Lake Michigan with the Mississippi River drainage. The amount of natural drainage involved would be inconsequential to the neighboring superstates, although the quantity of pollution originating in Chicago would continue to be, as now, of major importance.

CANADA
MICH.
N. DAK.
MINNESOTA
DULUTH
WISCONSIN
MINNEAPOLIS
ST. PAUL
S. DAK.
IOWA
CHICAGO
DES MOINES
OMAHA
NEBRASKA
ILLINOIS
IOWA
KANSAS CITY
ST. LOUIS
KANSAS
MISSOURI
MILES
0 100 250
0 100 350
KM.
49
95
90
45
45
40
40
98
37
37
90
94

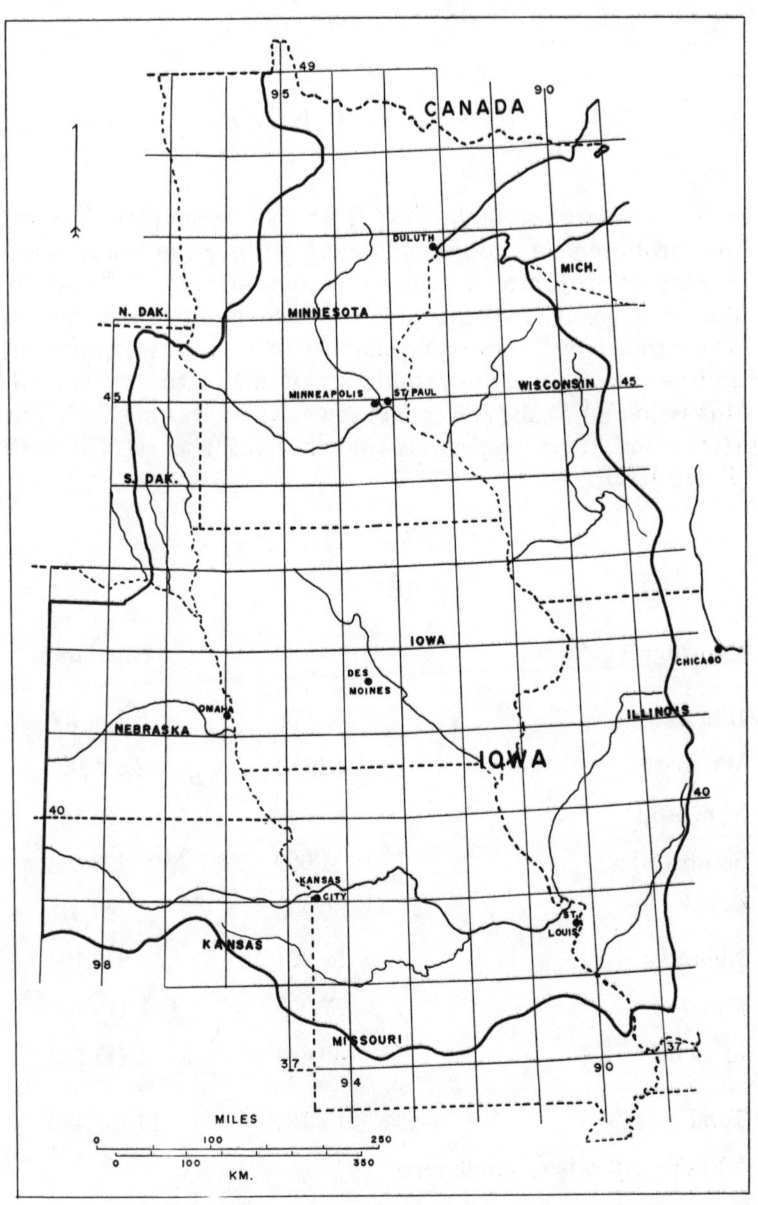

MAP NO. 4

IOWA—MAP NO. 4

Turn now to something at least a little simpler. Central to a proposed superstate and wholly included is Iowa, hence a very appropriate indigenous name to retain. Basically, the area covered is the upper Mississippi Valley, but in order to achieve reasonable equality in area plus population, and in view of the close similarity of the cultures involved, this is joined to the lower Missouri River Basin. The eight states and their respective contributions are set forth in Table VIII.

TABLE VIII
IOWA

Contributing States	Area—Sq. Mi.	Population
Illinois	38,900	3,302,456
Wisconsin	42,154	2,686,933
Minnesota	64,068	3,616,847
South Dakota	11,000	253,038
Iowa*	56,290	2,825,041
Nebraska	32,227	1,242,104
Kansas	27,000	1,119,768
Missouri	46,674	4,111,243
Total	318,313	19,157,430

* Entire. All others subdivided.

The area covered exceeds 300 thousand square miles; the population is more than 19 million, making it third in size and sixth in population, with an average density of 61 per square mile—only slightly below that of the entire United States. Here, if anywhere, is the typical *average* United States. Agriculture, based on corn especially, but amply assisted by soybeans, wheat, miscellaneous crops, and livestock, has laid the basis for a flourishing economy. Blessed with a temperate climate, rainfall generally adequate and suitably distributed to sustain agriculture without irrigation (mostly 30 to 40 inches annually), great areas of flatland with fertile soil suitable for large-scale farming, this region is the breadbasket and meat-store of the nation.

This is not to imply that conditions within this large subregion are by any means uniform. They vary from the range of the sweltering summer heat of St. Louis to the cool of the lakes and woodlands of northern Minnesota. The diminishing rainfall, westward, shades conditions gradually from the lush corn and bean fields of Illinois to the dry prairies of the Dakotas and central Nebraska. Indeed, it is a serious problem exactly where to draw the western boundaries, and this has generally been tailored as closely as possible to the line of 20 inches of annual rainfall, usually considered the absolute minimum to support agriculture without irrigation. Actual details of the boundary are modified to conform as much as possible with drainage basins. The Upper Missouri Basin, necessarily, is excluded because it would involve much too large an area, and in a region of very different natural characteristics and problems.

Mineral production in this region is substantial. Included are the very important iron ranges of northern Minnesota, a great bituminous coal center in southern and western Illinois, with others of less importance in Iowa, Missouri and Kansas; zinc-lead in southern Wisconsin and northern Illinois, and the world's largest lead-producing district on the southern margin—but here scheduled to be largely transferred to an adjacent superstate. This region also is a major source of barite. Clay deposits are worked extensively in central Missouri, and glass sand along the Mississippi River. Great cement works dot the Mississippi shores in Missouri and Illinois. Oil and gas are produced in minor volume in Kansas-Missouri and Missouri-Illinois.

Along with all these resources naturally goes a high degree of industrial development, with its inevitable patterns of pollution added to the normal problems of people, sewage, and drinking water. St. Louis, Kansas City, Omaha and Minneapolis-St. Paul are large manufacturing centers, with many smaller satellite cities specializing in a variety of products. Population, however, is not yet excessively concentrated into huge urban complexes, as it is particularly in Michigan and the northeastern trio of superstates. The large percentage of flat land with its high degree of cultivability should tend to perpetuate this condition. Pollution problems are serious but more solvable, probably, than in other regions, granted they could be concentrated into one managerial unit as here proposed rather than being scattered among eight separate authorities.

The inclusion of an outlet on Lake Superior in this unit was deliberate, as one of the aims of this proposed revamping of the United States has been to afford each component state, if at all possible, some direct outlet for ocean transportation. There was a question whether or not northern Minnesota should be included with Michigan in order to consolidate the Great Lakes even more effectively; or whether it should have been assigned to the hereafter-proposed inland superstate of Dakota in order to provide it with a deepwater outlet. However, the climatic conditions and economic ties of northern Minnesota seemed to favor its present disposition.

Owing once again to the dispersion of authority among so many separate state governments, the federalists have assumed primary control of the endless problems of flood control and navigation in the Missouri-Mississippi inland-waterway system. Much of this remote control might be dispensed with under the suggested reorganization. Presently rivers serve as state boundaries in some ten separate situations within the area, all of which could be eliminated in this rearrangement.

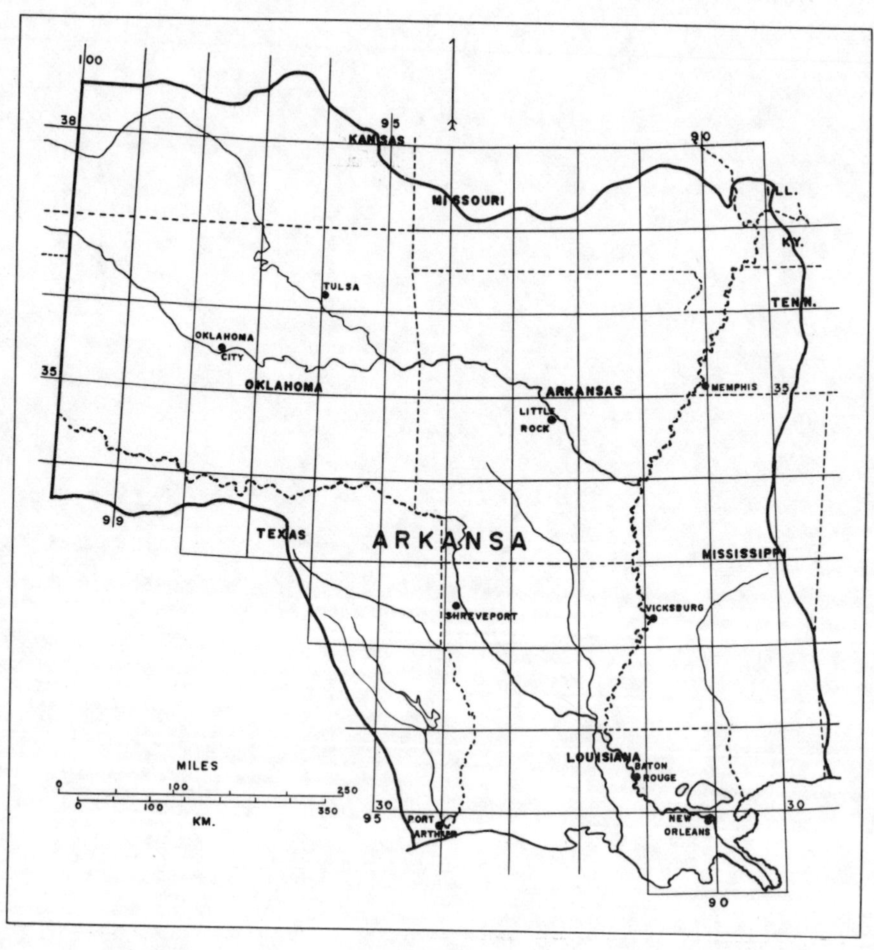

38
KANSAS
MISSOURI
95
90
ILL.
KY.
TENN.
TULSA
OKLAHOMA CITY
OKLAHOMA
35
ARKANSAS
MEMPHIS
35
LITTLE ROCK
99
TEXAS
ARKANSA
MISSISSIPPI
SHREVEPORT
VICKSBURG
LOUISIANA
BATON ROUGE
MILES
100
250
100
350
KM.
30
95
PORT ARTHUR
NEW ORLEANS
30
90

MAP NO. 5

ARKANSA—MAP NO. 5

Arkansa? Why bother with the extra "s," which has so long seemed to relegate *"Arkansaw"* to the backwoods? Especially when we are used to Kansas and use similar phonetics for the Arkansas River, one of its principal streams. It is suggested that Arkansa should match Arizona, Dakota, etc. in pronunciation. However, be that as it will. Small matter!

This superstate, centered around Arkansas, one of its two fully contained present entities, is constructed as shown in Table IX.

TABLE IX

ARKANSA

Contributing States	Area—Sq. Mi.	Population
Mississippi	41,216	1,997,323
Tennessee	8,500	1,106,763
Kentucky	1,000	52,740
Illinois	1,000	36,827
Missouri	23,000	566,156
Kansas	27,276	931,820
Oklahoma	63,919	2,532,474
Arkansas*	53,104	1,923,295
Texas	40,000	1,372,486
Louisiana*	48,523	3,643,180
Total	307,538	14,163,064

* Entire. All others subdivided.

Ten states contribute a total of 307,538 square miles with a population of 14,164,064, placing it fourth in area, seventh in population and ninth in density with 43 per square mile.

All the lower Mississippi River Basin is included up to points just above the Ohio-Mississippi confluence, plus all the two major tributaries, the Arkansas and Red rivers, entering from the west—except their comparatively arid headwaters, which constitute a separate problem. Likewise included are the basins of several minor rivers feeding directly into the Gulf in the Delta country. The intent has been to gather into one integrated unit all the lower Mississippi Valley area that is characterized by rainfall adequate for or in excess of the requirements for non-irrigated agriculture. Actually, with a rainfall generally of 30 inches or more over most of the north and west, increasing to nearly twice that amount in the south and east, the water problems of this region are largely those of flood control and drainage, plus, of course, pollution.

Some minor difficulties arise in choosing specific boundary lines on the west. In the Kansas-Oklahoma sector the 100th Meridian has been used as a convenient approximation to the line of demarcation characterized by 20 inches of annual rainfall. In addition to the Red River drainage in Texas, east of 100° w. longitude, all drainage of the Sabine and Neches rivers in east Texas has been included. This region, with more than ample rainfall, has characteristics and problems that seem more akin to those of Louisiana than of Texas, and the Sabine, like the Red River, now is in the awkward situation of constituting a state boundary and should be consolidated into one administrative unit. Texans, of course, doubtless will raise violent objections, but will have their compensations later.

Arkansa is basically an agricultural region, although it also has quite important mineral resources, including a large oil and gas production, important sulfur, and salt deposits, considerable coal of good bituminous quality in Arkansas and Oklahoma, important zinc-lead deposits in northeastern Oklahoma and elsewhere, plus, as the drainage divides dictate, a substantial part of the great southeastern Missouri lead district. In central Arkansas is the only important present source of aluminum ore within the United States, plus a major barite-producing district. Vanadium and copper are produced to some extent within the area, and still other products are or have been of minor importance. Altogether an impressive list.

However, as stated previously, the region is basically agricultural—and with its ample rainfall, long growing season, and generally deep soils, probably should remain so. Once the Land of Cotton, which is still important, it now produces cane sugar in large volume in Louisiana, rice in Arkansas, corn in various places, wheat extensively in Oklahoma and Kansas, fruit in the Ozark region, and cattle in many places. In opportunities for further agricultural development it rates high.

The Mississippi waterway, outlet to the sea not only for this but for the superstates of Ohio and Iowa to the north, naturally has invited the maximum of attention from the Corps of Engineers and the Federal Government with respect to navigation and flood control. This really is the only practical solution under the existing hodge-podge of divided state sovereignty. Six states are involved in the management of the great river within this area at present. Reducing this to one would be a great simplification, affording the possibility of eliminating most of the remote control from Washington. The minor problems of the Arkansas and Red rivers would be similarly simplified. All in all, Arkansa could be a really great and sovereign state.

Pollution problems in the area, until fairly recently, were somewhat less severe than in most other sections, due to the less advanced stages of industrialization and the relative abundance of water. Sewage disposal, however, lagged considerably behind many other regions. Lately, the rapidly developing wholesale use of insecticides in agriculture has introduced massive ecological maladjustments. Attempts to exterminate or control this or that pest for the benefit of certain agricultural interests have resulted in widespread decimation of beneficial species, in massive fish kills in rivers, etc. These problems could be handled advantageously if undertaken with determination, under the more centralized control that would be established by unification.

COLORADO
OKLA.
NEW MEXICO
TEXAS
TEXAS
MEXICO
LA.
DALLAS
HOUSTON
SAN ANTONIO
ALBUQUERQUE
EL PASO
MILES
KM.

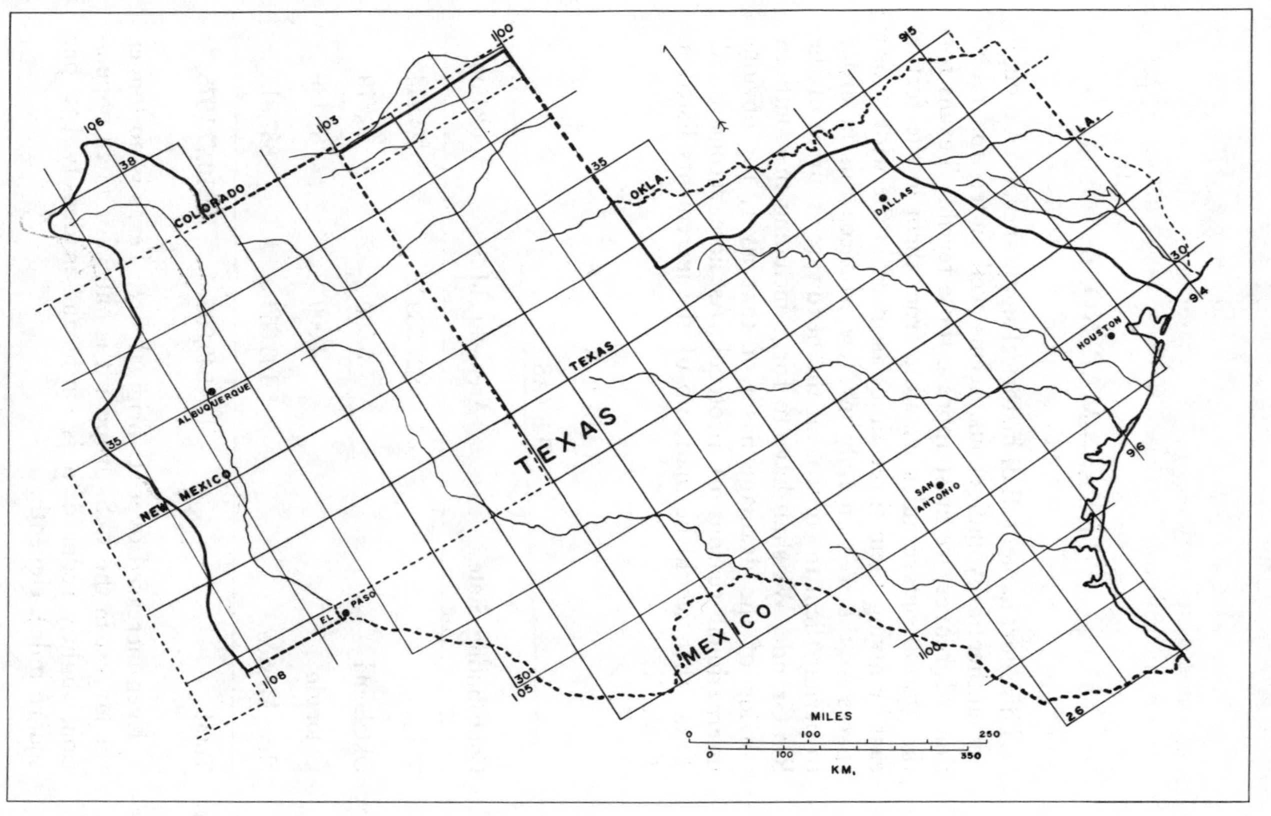

MAP NO. 6

TEXAS—MAP NO. 6

This short name, full of historical signficance, even though not authentically indigenous, seems well suited for retention. Moreover, we must appease those terrible Texans for the 37,000 square miles we stole from them in the fertile east by giving them three times as much in the wider open spaces of the west, mainly in New Mexico: this in order to permit them to control all the headwater sources of the Rio Grande. We shall have to forgo including the southern portion of the drainage basin of that river, for obvious international reasons of protocol. As here reconstituted, Texas then would be made up of the increments listed in Table X.

TABLE X

TEXAS

Contributing States	Area—Sq. Mi.	Population
Texas	227,339	9,824,244
Oklahoma	5,000	23,779
Colorado	4,000	37,139
New Mexico	103,666	887,813
Total	340,005	10,772,975

Even increased over its original size, Texas is no longer the largest in the U.S. proper; it is only No. 2! In population, slightly reduced, it is ninth, and in density (32 per square mile) eleventh.

Admittedly, this is a necessary compromise with various realities. First, as already stated, it covers only the United States portion of the Rio Grande Basin. Second, it includes the arid or semi-arid headwaters of various basins that drain eastward into Arkansa to become the Arkansas and Red rivers. These portions are so much more akin to western Texas in their cultural and climatic problems that they would be forgotten appendages of water-rich Arkansa— orphans, as the Panhandle of Oklahoma is now. Finally, Texas itself is a climatic compromise, combining a region of adequate or surplus rainfall in the southeast or Gulf slope with a considerably larger region of inadequate moisture in which agriculture can succeed only by means of irrigation. This situation is no different, except in degree, from that which exists already in Texas. It could be rectified by placing *all* the minor river basins tributary directly to the Gulf in Arkansa, but that would deprive the remainder of its principal outlets to the sea, as well as of the bulk of its population and an excessive portion of its economic resources. As it is, these balance out fairly well.

The southern portion of the Gulf slope of Texas is good agricultural country, without irrigation, devoted to such staples as cotton, corn, wheat, alfalfa, cattle, and, near the coast, citrus fruits and early vegetables. All up the Rio Grande Valley similar crops succeed under irrigation. The remaining, generally "high" country is mostly grazing land with some cultivation of wheat under dry-farming practice.

Dwarfing these products, however, in much of Texas, both low and high, are *oil* and *gas,* and the attendant industries that their abundance has attracted—chemicals, refineries, etc.—plus miscellaneous manufacturing enterprises. Along with oil, the Gulf Coast supplies salt and sulfur. The western mountains of Texas proper have yielded a minor quantity of minerals (mercury, silver), and the addition of the large areas in New Mexico would add very important resources in uranium, coal, and potash, as well as additional base metals, all tending to balance an economy presently overburdened by oil.

The problems of pollution in the industrialized southeast are severe, and the proposed restructuring of the state would do little to ameliorate this situation, which is already fully within the state's own borders. It would, however, simplify the control and utilization of the Rio Grande from its source to its mouth, and it would leave Texas as a better-balanced economic unit if and when the oil and gas wells ever run dry—which probably will happen some day, even though no Texan is likely to foresee such a possibility.

CANADA
114
110
105
100
95
49
49
GREAT FALLS
N. DAKOTA
BISMARCK
MINNESOTA
95
MONTANA
45
S. DAKOTA
45
IDAHO
PIERRE
WYOMING
NEBRASKA
110
OMAHA
96
DAKOTA
40
COLORADO
40
DENVER
4
MILES
0   100   250
KANSAS
0   100   350
KM.
37
37
105
OKLA.
100

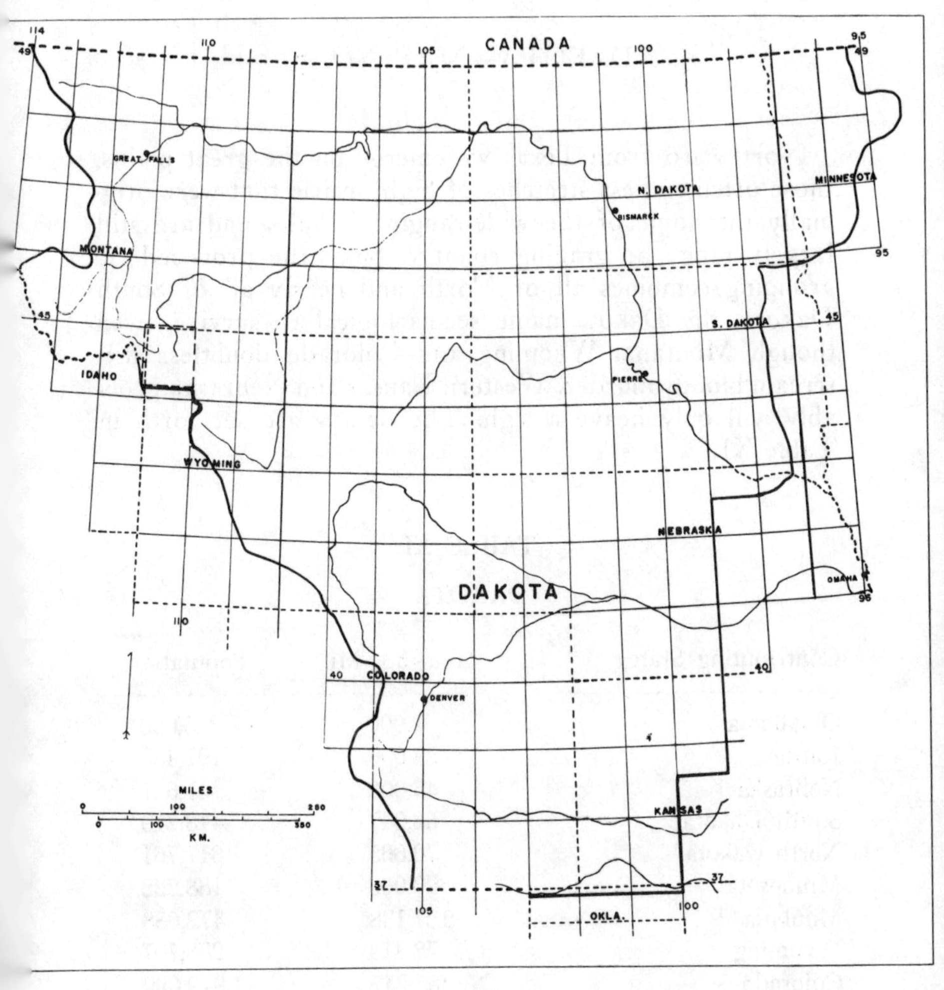

MAP NO. 7

Northward from Texas we emerge on the great plains, those often endless stretches of high prairie that were originally the home of the wide-ranging buffalo, and are still largely range or grazing country. Since the proposed regrouping combines all of North and nearly all of South Dakota, the Dakota name seems logical to survive, even though Montana, Wyoming and Colorado doubtless will scream bloody murder. Western Kansas and Nebraska probably will only heave a sigh. The details are set forth in Table XI.

TABLE XI

DAKOTA

Contributing States	Area—Sq. Mi.	Population
Oklahoma	1,000	3,000
Kansas	28,000	197,483
Nebraska	45,000	241,687
South Dakota	66,047	413,219
North Dakota*	70,665	617,761
Minnesota	20,000	188,222
Montana	127,138	472,688
Wyoming	72,414	288,707
Colorado	65,247	1,979,099
Total	495,511	4,401,866

* Entire. All others subdivided.

In addition to the seven states already mentioned, a considerable area in Minnesota is included to consolidate the valley of the Red River of the North, which, as a prairie wheat and sugar beet country, is allied more to the west than to the Minnesota forest belt. Likewise, a tiny strip of the panhandle of Oklahoma is taken in to cover the headwaters of a minor and generally waterless drainage system. The entire region is part of the Mississippi Valley Basin, tributary for the most part to the Missouri River. The eastern border is tailored approximately to the 20-inch line of annual rainfall, marking as nearly as possible the borderline of irrigated versus non-irrigated agriculture, although this distinction is far from exact.

The western boundary, of necessity, is the Continental Divide, since the objective is to place within one jurisdiction all sources of natural water supply for this highly water-deficient area, most of which receives only 10 to 15 inches of annual precipitation, some areas even less. However, a relatively narrow but irregular belt on the west, just east of the Great Divide, and vastly different topographically from the dominating great plains, consists of the rugged Rocky Mountain front; and this receives, in very erratic distribution, a considerably greater annual precipitation up to perhaps 40 inches in some places. This falls, moreover, largely as winter snow and, by gradual melting, nurtures the perennial flow of many still comparatively pure mountain streams. It is essential that this scanty water supply be doled out and utilized with the utmost care; and the consolidation of this unduly large but generally culturally homogenous region should facilitate greatly the equitable solution of its pressing problems.

As it is, the proposed superstate covers almost 500,000 square miles, one sixth of the United States proper, yet contains only 4.4 million people—a density of but nine per square mile, making it easily 13th in both population total and density.

Economically the region is primarily oriented agriculturally, with the emphasis on cattle and wheat, the latter cul-
tivated mainly as a dry-farming crop utilizing to the best
possible advantage the scanty seasonal moisture of winter
and early spring. Along narrow stretches of valleys some
irrigation is practiced to produce other crops, such as corn
and alfalfa. Non-tillable and non-irrigable range land supports a sparse distribution of range livestock, mainly cattle.

The mountain country on the west, much of it forested,
has a considerably different economy that usually mixes
ranching and agriculture in the valleys with forestry, mining
and recreation catering to tourists and vacationers, both
summer and winter.

In mineral resources the region has a wide variety, including numerous oil and gas fields generally of limited productivity, and scattered coal—of bituminous quality in southern
Colorado and Wyoming, and of poor lignitic quality in
North Dakota. Gold, silver, copper, lead and zinc are
important at various places in the Rockies, especially Colorado and Montana. Uranium is important in Colorado
and Wyoming. The Black Hills, which break the monotony
of the great plains in South Dakota, long have been famous
for the Homestake gold mine and minor amounts of other
minerals.

Industrially, the lack of water greatly hampers development, not by any means a total misfortune. The sparse population tends to ease the problems of pollution to some
degree; but, nevertheless, the severe shortage of water, especially seasonally, renders it difficult to dispose of sewage.
Artesian water is utilized extensively for domestic uses and
stock, even locally for irrigation, though this may easily
overtax the supply. Flood control within the area itself is
generally no serious problem except very locally; but the
Corps of Engineers has found it desirable, nevertheless, to
establish great reservoirs on the Upper Missouri for the
purpose of reducing the impact of floods on the lower
reaches of the Missouri-Mississippi complex, as well as to

provide for regulation of the flow in dry periods for the benefit of navigation.

Dakota is the only proposed superstate with no access to effective water transportation. This situation could have been avoided, as previously suggested, by giving it a corridor to the head of Lake Superior along the northern edge of Minnesota, but this seemed to necessitate adding an area of too radically different characteristics to a region already overlarge.

The advantages of combining these several states and portions of states should be obvious. Surely western Kansas and Nebraska would feel more at home and have their interests better served by joining with the very similar regions of the Dakotas, Colorado and Wyoming, than by remaining, as now, overshadowed and neglected by their far more populous and more richly endowed eastern segments. Unification would strengthen the state governmental structure by enlarging its scope and resources, so that more effective departments of education, transportation, water supply and mineral resources could replace weak and inadequate or non-existent bureaus of the present structures of some of these states.

Dakota as thus conceived epitomizes the transcendent importance of water supply with respect to the land's capacity to support human habitation. With a total area of nearly 500,000 square miles, it is almost identical in size to the combined five superstates of Michigan, Ohio, Chesapeak, Mohawk and Merimak (497,520 square miles), that is virtually all the region east of the Mississippi River occupying latitudinal limits similar to those of "Dakota." With 10 to 15 inches of annual rainfall the Dakota region receives approximately one-third as much precipitation as the northeastern United States, which averages only slightly above 30 inches per annum. Moreover, the Dakota area, with its nearly limitless flat plains, contains much more potentially arable land than the East, where large areas are moderately rugged and extensively forested. Yet Dakota supports pres-

67

ently only 4.4 million people, whereas the northeast teems with 100 millions!

One may well raise the question as to whether or not such a small population, in spite of the large area it represents, deserves consideration as a separate state. The author's conclusion is, however, that its distinctive characteristics and unique problems demand unified control; and its potentialities—assuming the possibility that at least partial solutions to its water shortage eventually may be developed either through climate control, chemical purification processes, or diversion from regions of excess supply, such as the westerly slopes of the Rockies or even the Far North in Canada—are ample to justify it as a separate entity.

With respect to water diversions, however, it may be noted that several such programs already are in effect. The Denver, Colorado, area for many years has augmented its water supply by diversion of Colorado River Basin water from west of the Continental Divide through the privately constructed Moffatt Tunnel. More recently the United States Reclamation Service has created three other much larger diversion projects, also in the State of Colorado. Such diversions necessarily reduce the amount of water available for the even more arid region of Arizona. Considering the extreme importance and value of water as illustrated in an earlier paragraph, it would seem only proper that such diversions should not be made heedlessly. They should be compensated financially at rates or on terms much more generous than usually has been customary in the past. Even granted that the water so diverted may be potentially of more value in the area of proposed deflection, where possibly it can be put to use nearer its source and with less loss from evaporation, etc., this only enhances its intrinsic value to both parties.

110
43
WYOMING
SALT LAKE CITY
UTAH
COLORADO
40
106
115
N. MEXICO
35
NEVADA
ARIZONA
CALIFORNIA
35
PHOENIX
ARIZONA
LOS ANGELES
TUCSON
119
31
SAN DIEGO
110
MEXICO
31
115
MILES
0
100
250
0
100
350
KM.

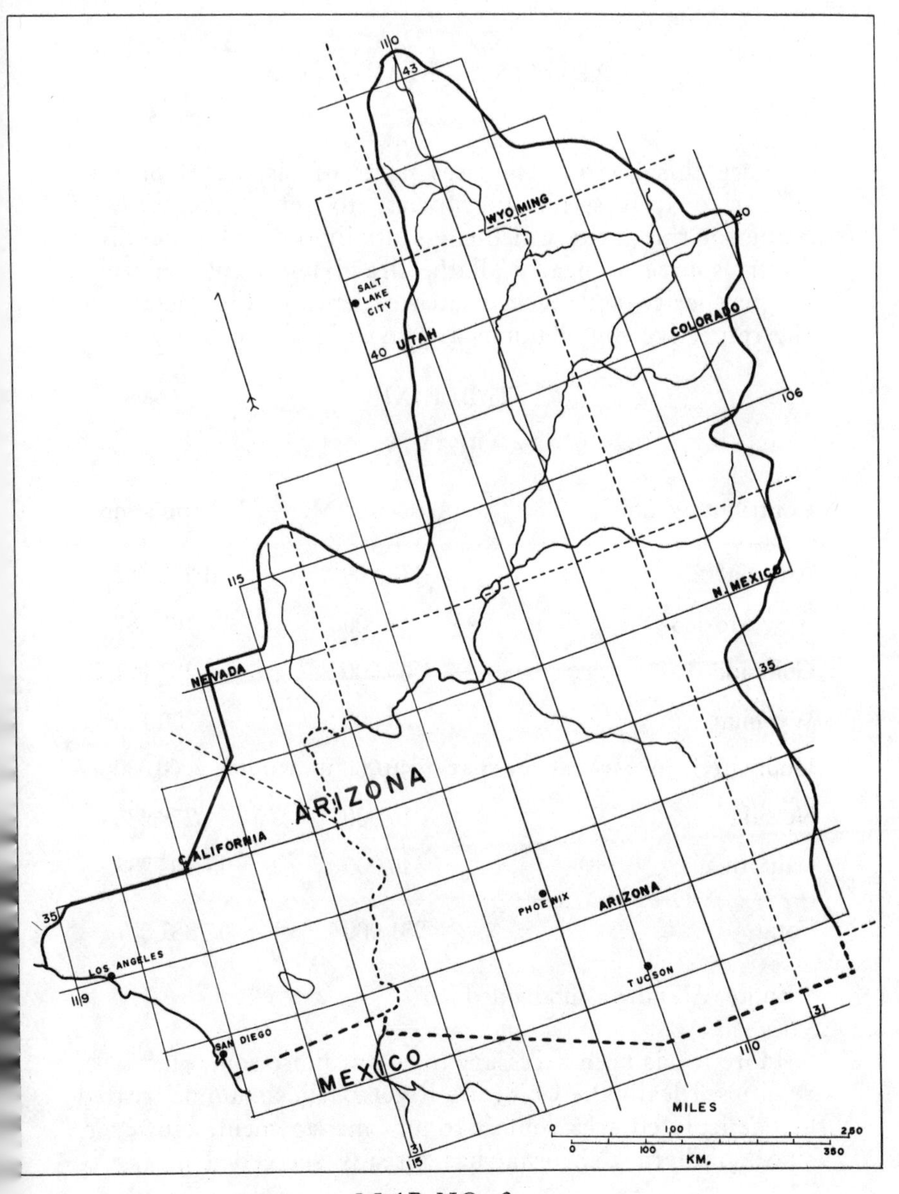

MAP NO. 8

Since this region comprises parts of six states plus all of Arizona, it seems appropriate to retain the Arizona name for this entity which is essentially the Colorado River Basin, source of nearly all the life-giving water on which its prosperity and even existence depend. The details of the respective contributions are given in Table XII.

TABLE XII

ARIZONA

Contributing States	Area—Sq. Mi.	Population
Arizona*	113,909	1,772,482
New Mexico	18,000	128,187
Colorado	35,000	191,021
Wyoming	20,000	30,146
Utah	45,000	79,330
Nevada	10,000	276,288
California	40,000	11,404,383
Total	281,909	13,881,837

* Entire. All others subdivided.

Here it has been necessary to compromise somewhat with realities. Ideally the Colorado River Basin should be treated as one isolated area subject to unit management. However, since southern California has already succeeded in appropriating a large portion of its water supply and diverting much of this outside the Colorado Basin to support the grossly overgrown population of the small Los Angeles Basin, which is woefully short of water for its vastly over-industrialized economy, there appears to be no solution other than to accept this regrettable situation and combine the two areas into one superstate. Actually, this procedure makes sense in that it produces a state which is superficially well balanced in area (fifth), in population (eighth), and in average density (also eighth, at 49 per square mile). These figures, however, mask the fact that one-seventh of the area, in California, contained four-fifths of the nearly 14 million population in 1970. Nevertheless, as with so many of our festering urban problems, the facts must be coped with as they are. The suggested combination seems logical and workable, and should be a great improvement over the present situation in which compacts involving at least six states are necessary to achieve any legal distribution of the Colorado's water—a situation which has led to federal control and operation of the extensive Colorado River development projects. To some degree this has been because of the international aspect affecting agreements with Mexico regarding the share of water it should receive, since the natural discharge of the Colorado is in Mexican territory, although all the water originates in the United States.

Most of the outlines of the Colorado basin are clear-cut. However, minor problems arise in the desert areas of Nevada and southern California, where there is no run-off, but only ephemeral drainage into closed interior basins. For this area straight-line boundaries are suggested which could be varied as circumstances might warrant.

The superstate of Arizona then would embrace the following principal components:

1. The densely populated and highly industrialized Los Angeles-San Diego coastal margin, a region of (formerly) ideal climate with moderate rainfall in the range of 20

71

inches per annum, received mainly in winter and spring months. Here citrus cultivation once was a major industry. Oil, aircraft and other factories, people, and automobiles have turned this one-time paradise into a modern poison-pit.

2. The "Imperial" Valley, a small area in southeastern California, which, in spite of a nearly insufferable summer climate of heat and desert dryness has, by irrigation from the Colorado River, become a veritable Garden of Eden for the production of vegetables, fruits, high-grade cotton, alfalfa, etc., widely marketed throughout the United States.

3. Similar areas in Arizona intensively developed agriculturally along irrigable valleys, with more emphasis on citrus fruits and cotton, and alfalfa.

4. North of the Imperial Valley, in southern California (Palm Springs) and southern Nevada (Las Vegas) and on the great artificial impoundments of the Colorado (Lake Mead, etc.), a winter playground for rich and poor, for Hollywood stars, Mafia bosses, and ex-Presidents. In this area rainfall is, for practical purposes, virtually unknown— possibly 3 to 7 inches per year, mainly in sudden local showers.

5. In the southern two-thirds of Arizona and adjoining New Mexico, a great mineral complex based primarily on copper mining, intensively developed at many separate centers with smelting facilities going hand-in-hand. Gold, silver and molybdenum are by-products, plus smog, not yet to match Los Angeles, but with the assistance of increasing industrialization (factories, etc.) tending rapidly in that direction.

6. On the upper Colorado above Lake Mead, the Grand Canyon country, a scenic wonderland of worldwide fame and attraction, which is being swiftly conquered by dams

and highways to render it continually more accessible to the public and less attractive to the individual. In this region there is only very limited cultivation of minor valleys where water is available and occasional widely scattered, small mining operations, with some exceptions as noted hereafter.

7. In addition to copper, less grandiose mining operations are widely scattered over almost the entire area. Presently most important perhaps is uranium mining, which centers around the "Four Corners" where Colorado, New Mexico, Utah and Arizona meet. The mountain uplifts of the Continental Divide in Colorado and of the Wasatch Divide in Utah contain numerous deposits of gold, silver, lead, zinc, copper, etc. that are being or have been exploited on various scales; and similar but generally small operations, past or present, dot the scattered mountain ranges of western New Mexico, Arizona and southern California.

Climatically, most of Arizona is natural desert with less than 10 inches of annual precipitation, especially at low altitudes. Mountain or plateau heights receive somewhat more, up to 20 or more inches locally, and may sustain forest cover. The high ranges of the great divides receive much more, up to 40 inches or higher, mainly as winter snow which, by summer melting, maintains the life-giving flow of the Colorado. The utilization and distribution of this precious resource is the prime economic and political problem of the region, and thus justifies, even demands, its unification. In addition, the area has increasingly in common the pervasive necessity of coping with atmospheric smog which is already decimating the mountain pine forests of California and threatens ultimately to asphyxiate the human population in ghastly retribution for careless over-development.

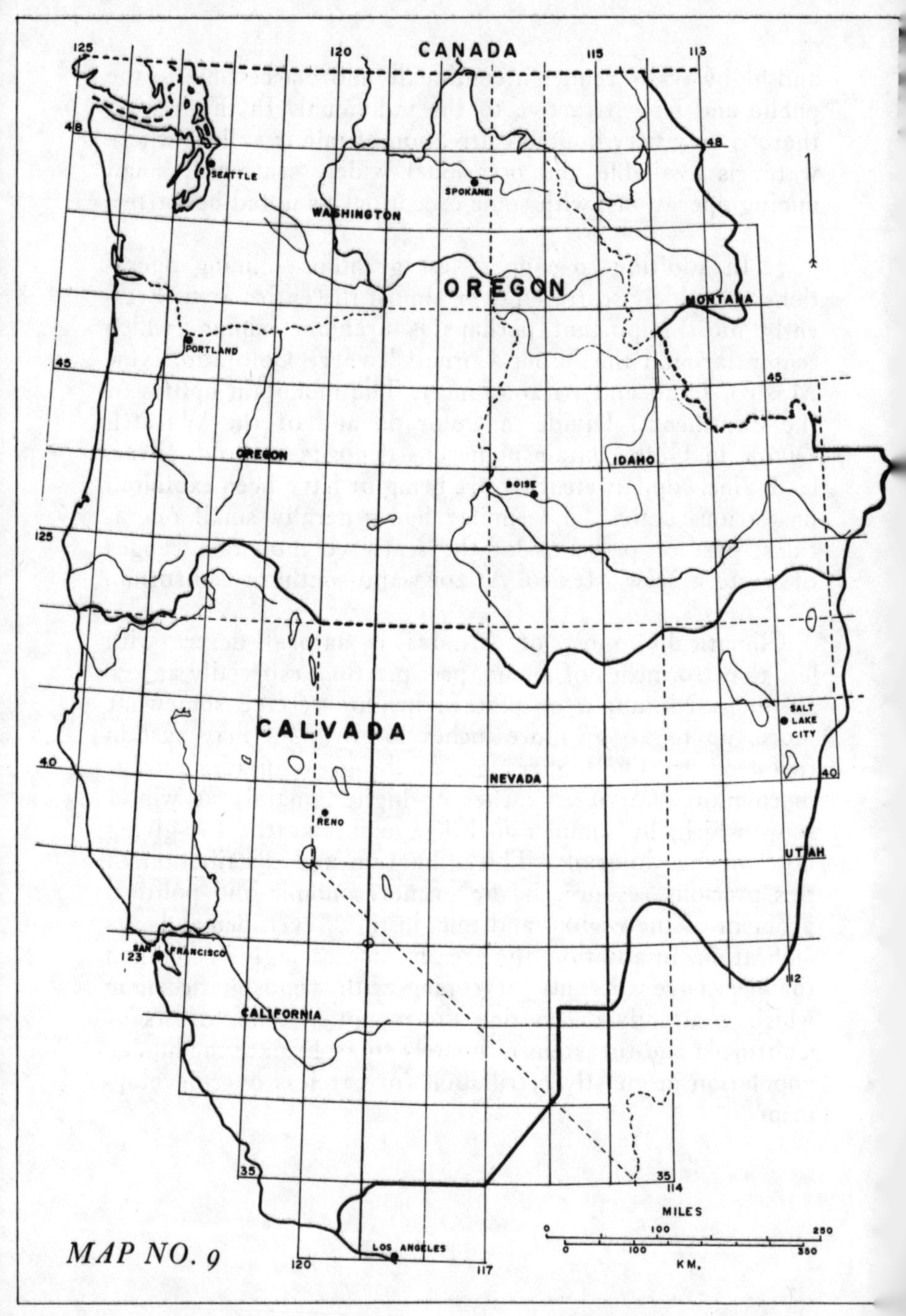

CANADA
125
120
115
113
48
48
SEATTLE
SPOKANE
WASHINGTON
OREGON
MONTANA
PORTLAND
45
45
OREGON
IDAHO
BOISE
125
SALT
LAKE
CITY
CALVADA
40
NEVADA
40
RENO
UTAH
SAN FRANCISCO
123
112
CALIFORNIA
35
35
114
MILES
0
100
250
0
100
350
KM.
120
LOS ANGELES
117
MAP NO. 9

CALVADA—MAP NO. 9

Nevada is a Spanish inheritance—the Sierra Nevada being the snowy mountains, though conspicuous only in winter. *California* likewise is Spanish in origin, but of rather legendary and uncertain connotation. The abridgement is suggested as a suitable name for this superstate, consisting mainly of California, minus the Los Angeles area and southeastern desert, plus Nevada, with western Utah thrown in. Details are set forth in Table XIII.

TABLE XIII
CALVADA

Contributing States	Area—Sq. Mi.	Population
California	118,693	8,548,751
Nevada	97,540	211,450
Utah	39,916	979,943
Oregon	5,500	54,021
Idaho	3,000	16,038
Wyoming	1,500	6,100
Total	266,149	9,816,303

Almost as large as Arizona, this superstate ranks seventh in area, tenth in population with nearly ten million people, and tenth in average density at 37 per square mile. However, since more than three-fourths of this population is concentrated in approximately one-fourth of the area in the great central valley and along the coast of California, and one-half the remainder in a relatively small north-south belt centered on Salt Lake City, the regional contrasts are extreme. Indeed, the population in the large Nevada contribution of space is only slightly more than two per square mile! This reflects very naturally the wide extremes of climate, and especially of water supply. California west of the Sierra Divide receives variously from 20 inches per annum in the south and at low altitudes to more than 40 in the north, graded proportionally to altitude and latitude between these extremes. Again, in this Mediterranean-type coastal climate most of the moisture comes in winter or early spring, and irrigation, sustained by water storage, is essential for agriculture.

Once a prime agricultural storehouse and source of superlative fruits and vegetables plus grain crops and alfalfa, the fertile great central valley of northern California is rapidly nearing the same degree of desolation and destruction by over-development, residentially and industrially, that plagues southern California.

The eastern margin of California, all of Nevada except its mountain peaks, and Utah west of Salt Lake are typical interior desert, with generally less than 10 inches of precipitation that falls, largely as snow in the winter months, on the higher western slopes of the Wasatch Mountains. Utilized in irrigation, this nurtures a secondary outpost of modern population and industrial concentration, essentially similar to but much smaller than that in California .and with a much wider range of climatic variation from summer to winter.

There may be some question as to whether this western Utah region should be attached to Calvada as proposed, or should have been awarded to Arizona, much of which it closely resembles in cultural and economic development; but the present mode of assignment makes for better balance in area and population, and fits well with the close ties between Salt Lake City and San Francisco in transportation and financial orientation. However, the matter is debatable.

Aside from its basic irrigated agricultural base, Calvada possesses many other valuable resources. Western Utah and Nevada, like Arizona, contain numerous major copper deposits that are exploited on the largest scales, accompanied by smelting operations and benefitting from recoverable by-products. The Great Salt Lake itself is a vast storehouse of valuable mineral salines that are increasingly commercialized. The Salt Lake Valley supports a modest iron and steel industry buttressed by plentiful Utah coal. Large lead-zinc mines are exploited, albeit not as continuously as with copper mining. Gold was important in the past primarily in California, as was silver in Nevada and Utah, and a small amount of gold still is produced, mainly in Nevada. Copper was formerly of some importance in California and may be again. Coastal California contains almost the only mercury mines of any importance in the United States. Oil and gas are important in the southern part of California's great valley, as well as, sad to say, offshore. There are possibilities that they may yet be discovered in significant amounts in Nevada and Utah.

Finally, recreation, or tourism, based on a fundamentally delightful climate and magnificent scenery, is a highly merchantable asset the year around. Its over-promotion is one of the sadder aspects of the debasement of Utopia.

Since, for better or worse, the world is as it is, we have to make the best of it. It is believed that the proposed superstate would be adequately endowed and better organized to manage its pressing internal problems under the reorganization here proposed. Nevada could become part of a viable superstate rather than attempting to exist, as now, dependent extensively on gambling, divorce and similar degrading activities for its livelihood. Attached to California, it could serve that area as a useful haven of escape

in hours of stress. As for the separation of northern from
southern California, it is doubtful that the populace of
either area would feel much regret at its escape from in-
volvement with the other.

Our last superstate combines all of Washington, most of both Oregon and Idaho, and a sizable chunk of Montana. Since it seems scarcely appropriate to honor George Washington with the name of a superstate, the present state being often needlessly confused with the nation's capital anyway, the good indigenous name of "Oregon" is appropriate for retention. Admittedly, "Idaho" would be equally acceptable, but on the basis of relative importance Oregon deserves the honor. Table XIV gives the details of area and population.

Only slightly larger than Calvada in area, the new superstate is firmly in twelfth place in population (over six million) and average density (24 per square mile), which places it next to its eastern neighbor, Dakota, as the least

TABLE XIV
OREGON

Contributing States	Area—Sq. Mi.	Population
Oregon	91,481	2,037,364
Idaho	80,557	696,970
Wyoming	4,000	7,463
Montana	20,000	221,721
Nevada	3,000	1,000
Washington*	68,192	3,409,169
Total	267,230	6,373,687

* Entire. All others subdivided.

congested part of the United States. This condition it undoubtedly will strive manfully to improve (?) by increasing its people and thereby its problems.

Basically, this state, like Arizona, consists mainly of a single basin, that of the Columbia River, except for a minor portion which lies across the international boundary in Canada. A small area in Washington drains directly into Puget Sound, and additional small areas on the western slopes of the coast ranges feed directly into the sea in Oregon and Washington.

Climatically the proposed superstate is similar to its southern neighbors in varying widely from the coast inland, but on the average is better-watered and cooler. The coastal ranges are copiously watered with 40 inches in the south to 60 or more in the north, sufficient to maintain a virtual rain-forest type of vegetation on the Olympic Peninsula. Again, the rain falls much more abundantly in winter, but the sea moderates the temperature so as to yield little snow near the coast. Inland is a different matter, and Mount Rainier and other heights to the east of the coastal valleys receive copious winter snow. Centrally, rainfall diminishes to 10 to 20 inches and semi-desert conditions prevail over large areas, especially of the Columbia River lava plateaus. In the mountains of northern Idaho and the adjacent Flathead country of Montana, winter snow abounds and broad areas are heavily forested. Much of southern Idaho, at lower elevations, is again semi-desert. Even in the coastal valleys south of Seattle and Portland the lessened rainfall at low altitudes and its seasonal nature, falling mainly in winter, necessitate irrigation for successful agriculture. The agricultural base of the economy as a whole, therefore, is still heavily dependent on water control to facilitate irrigation. And to provide power! For the Columbia River system with its large volume of water, fed in summer by the melting snows but diminishing in winter, even though that is the rainy season—forming as it does state boundaries in two localities (Washington-Oregon; Oregon-Idaho) and deriving its water from four states plus Canada—has been a natural object for federal control and development, as at the great Bonneville Dam. This is supplemented by numerous private power-company developments elsewhere. Once more, the unification of this several-state complex into one governmental unit would simplify its operation and provide a far better-diversified economic base than now exists for any single state.

The forest resources of this superstate, in the coast ranges, and in the northern Idaho-Montana sector, are perhaps the most valuable in the nation. Its fisheries, although imminently threatened by pollution and power developments, if they can be saved, are of supreme importance. Its agriculture, based on wheat, small grains, potatoes, fruits and alfalfa, is very important and capable of considerable expansion. Its mineral resources are large, including the great copper mines of Butte, Montana, almost on the Continental Divide, the noted lead-zinc-silver mining complex of the Coeur-d'Alenes in northern Idaho, an important zinc-lead district in northeastern Washington, plus copper, nickel and other minerals elsewhere, and a scattering of gold and silver mines, past or potential, in numerous other localities, particularly southern Idaho and Oregon.

Add to these the superb port facilities of Puget Sound, ideal for trans-Pacific and Alaska-bound traffic, plus additional facilities on the lower Columbia at Portland, and top off with the whipped cream of unsurpassed scenic and recreational facilities, again summer and winter, and we have an enviable ensemble worthy of the most careful nurturing and preservation.

Sad to say, the problems of pollution by industrial wastes, human refuse, and shipping residues already loom large in Puget Sound and the lower Columbia River. Here also the specter of air pollution hovers over these idyllic valleys. May they never repeat the blunders that have desecrated southern California and ominously threaten the San Francisco area!

POLITICAL, SOCIAL AND ECONOMIC DIVIDENDS OF REORGANIZATION

1. Representation

Surely there can be no question that political representation in the national government would be much more equitable and realistic and should be more effective under the proposed reorganization than at present. Where is there any justice when two senators from Nevada, or Wyoming, or Vermont, representing less than 500,000 people, have an equal voice with two from California, representing 20 million? This inequity is repeated in milder form in the Electoral College, where each national legislator (senator or congressman) counts for one electoral vote. It operates much more seriously, though less obviously, in the Constitutional provision that the legislatures of *three-fourths of the states* must ratify an amendment to the constitution. This sets up a situation in which thirteen states—Delaware, Idaho, Maine, Montana, New Hampshire, Nevada, North Dakota, Rhode Island, South Dakota, Vermont, Wyoming, Alaska and Hawaii, each with a population of less than one million (four with less than half a million), or a total of less than 10 million people—can thwart the will of 200 millions; a ratio of only five per cent compared to the twenty-five per cent contemplated in the Constitution.

Perhaps least importantly, yet regrettably, the nature of politics dictates that because small states have few electoral votes their citizens, no matter how able or well qualified, can almost never hope to attain the Presidency. How many Presidents have come from the list of thirteen small states just enumerated? None, except by the expedient of removal to a larger power-base (e.g., Calvin Coolidge from Vermont to Massachusetts). But New York, with its huge electoral vote, has supplied at least half a dozen. Admittedly some of these were men of distinction and ability, such as the two Roosevelts and Grover Cleveland. But would Van Buren or Fillmore or Arthur ever have been likely prospects had they not had this advantage? And how many also-rans have been nominated for the Presidency or Vice-Presidency simply because of the geography and politics of their residence in New York or some similarly important state? This situation tempts likely candidates to shift residences, as with the late Senator Robert Kennedy, or even to establish virtually multiple citizenship in important states. Who knows, offhand, what state is entitled to claim Richard Nixon as its contribution to the Presidency? New York? Or California? Or even Florida?

2. *Law-Enforcement*

A prime benefit from the suggested enlargement of the states and revision of their boundaries should be a vast improvement in the operability of law-enforcement. The present small size of many states, complicated by their crazy-quilt boundaries and the growth of huge urban complexes along and across these boundaries in many places, seems diabolically contrived to enable criminals to escape swiftly from one jurisdiction to another, for shysters to take advantage of lenient provisions in the laws of one state compared to its neighbors, or even to corrupt the legal functioning of weak and thinly populated states adjacent to rich and wealthy ones (e.g., Nevada-California, etc.) It even facilitates unnecessarily and inequitably a tendency for wealthy individuals or corporations deriving their income mainly from from some larger state or states to shelter it in the tax haven of neighbors less civic-minded or less urgently beset financially (e.g., New York vs. New Jersey or Delaware).

The restriction of police from crossing state boundaries, the complications of extradition proceedings for criminals, etc., the multiplicity of labor laws and building codes, all are conditions that should be vastly improved under reorganization. The mere reduction of automobile licenses from forty-eight to thirteen in the continental United States is a dramatic illustration of the potentialities for simplification, with the doubled dividends of increased efficiency in law-enforcement and a reduction in its cost.

3. *Taxation*

In the field of taxation there should be rich rewards of efficiency and economy *provided the necessary readjustments of responsibility and means are met.* As the country now operates, very few states have sufficient area, population, resources, and varieties of resources to smooth the impact of economic cycles and "acts of God" such as hurricanes, earthquakes, droughts, floods, etc., and to be really sovereign. Many are so small, weak and limited in range of productivity that they cannot possibly be self-supporting. The inevitable result is that the Federal Government steps in where the states abrogate their duties to supply or administer disaster relief, welfare obligations, educational requirements, highway and transportation facilities, sewage and pollution control, housing and urban redevelopment, etc., etc. To do this the Federal Government must control and has pre-empted the most productive sources of revenue, leaving the states only lesser sources with little margin on which to depend. Thus the federal income tax, yielding seventy-five percent of all national income, has grown so large that the states, even though they can legally and in many cases do levy a similar tax, cannot possibly hope to compete with Washington without either wrecking their economies or inciting rebellion. The Federal Government alone collects duties on imports, a source not available to the states. It also levies many excise taxes, such as on liquor, tobacco, gasoline, etc., which the states may escalate, but again only at the risk of economic dislocation, and often under prohibitive difficulty of enforcement due largely to the intricate complexity and number of state boundaries.

The proposed reorganization of states, or some similar rearrangement and simplification, would give each super-state adequate space, population and range of resources to handle most of these programs itself without first remitting the taxes to Washington and then having to plead abjectly for their return, minus the inevitable overhead and incident delay, not to mention the political in-fighting always attendant on such programs.

Obviously, to make the rearrangement work the Federal Government would have to cede to the states requisite sources of revenue, say for instance *50 per cent of all income taxes*—the Federal Government to set the rate, and the state to have the privilege of rebating to its citizens if desired but *not* of increasing the levy. The levying of tariffs or import-export duties probably should remain entirely in federal hands, and no state should be permitted to lay tariffs on interstate or foreign commerce. States, however, should have full control over excise and property taxes within their borders and the Federal Government might need the power to lay tariffs on interstate commerce. The foregoing are only random ideas. The details necessarily should be worked out by economists, with legal assistance.

4. Industrial Control

Here, really, is the heart of the problem. Since each superstate would be virtually the equivalent of a nation (larger than many important existing ones), it should be completely self-supporting in all but matters of foreign policy and national defense. It should build and maintain its own highways, police and supervise its river systems and coastal waters (say, to the three-mile limit), build and operate or regulate its airfields subject to federal interstate safety requirements, support or stifle its own educational institutions as it might choose, regulate and distribute its water supplies and be accountable for their purity or pollution, care for its cities and its poor without help or hindrance from Washington, and in short, be really sovereign and equal. This it could do without the endless lost motion, red tape and overhead expense of administration from afar. Since air pollution, including radiation effects, still would transgress state lines, some federal control or minimum standards probably should be established, but with the states permitted to add greater safeguards as might be necessary, especially in congested areas.

5. The Federal Structure

One of the prime objectives of this proposal is to deflate the awkward and inefficient federal structure, already colossally overgrown, returning to the localities concerned all functions dealing with local problems, and freeing the federal apparatus to fulfill its proper role of managing foreign relations, national defense, and similar matters affecting the nation as a whole. Thus the Interior Department could be, for all practical purposes, disbanded, its functions returned to the states in which they are exercised. Public lands should be returned to the states for individual management, even though this might at first invite even more rapacious exploitation than at present. There are states (e.g., New York) which already set precedents the Federal Government might well emulate in the management of public lands, and experience should be a helpful teacher to others. One exception might be a system of National Parks situated strictly along state boundaries, such as Yellowstone and the Smokies. These might well be expanded.

The Corps of Engineers, with all its pork-barrel activities, should be abolished. Only a simple compact between four states (Arkansa, Ohio, Iowa and Dakota) would be required to manage even the entire Mississippi-Missouri Basin, and all others are self-contained.

The Department of Agriculture, like the Interior, would be virtually superfluous. Each state would control sufficient area, and usually of rather unique character distinctive from other states, to enable it to manage its particular problems to better advantage than by dependence on Washington. Production control of specific major crops, usually likely to be of predominant importance in one, or at most a few states, should be regulated by the states just as oil production now is pro-rated in various places. The enlargement of states and reduction of interstate boundaries would lend itself to much more effective control of the problem of insect infestation and plant diseases and their spread across state boundaries, as effective check-stations could be established more easily and uniformly.

The Departments of Health, Education and Welfare, and Housing and Urban Development would be superfluous; and, for the most part, Transportation also, except for problems of interstate railroad and air traffic. Commerce should deal strictly with foreign commerce. Labor? This is really a hot potato! Surely drastic curbs on the existing piratical powers and policies of nationally organized unions are overdue. Perhaps states should be permitted to handle this subject with complete autonomy. Justice? Another conundrum. Corporations are scarcely less plunder-minded than unions. In fact, they contributed to bringing the present one-sided labor laws upon their own heads by rapacious and restrictive policies. Clearly, the Federal Government would still have to attempt to dispense or assure even-handed justice. The Post Office? Even now, almost everybody without a finger in the pie believes it would be better off as a private enterprise.

How could the proposed revamping of state structures be made palatable to existing institutions? Senatorial representation is a major stumbling-block. This, it would seem, might be solved readily by giving each superstate an increased number of senators somewhere in the range from six to nine. For states with very small populations, such as Hawaii and Alaska, a reasonable restriction to something proportionate to population would be in order—say one or two senators, to be increased if and when population statistics should justify such a move. Certainly the allotment of six to nine senators to such small segments of the population would be an absurdity, even though scarcely worse than that of our existing disparities.

WASHINGTON, THE NATIONAL CAPITAL

During the birth of the United States from 1774 to 1800, the representatives of the thirteen colonies, assembled as the Continental Congress and later as the Congress of the United States, met hither and thither, in Baltimore, Philadelphia, New York, and various other places, but particularly in Philadelphia and New York. In 1790 the Congress accepted an invitation tendered in substantially the same form by the states of Maryland and Virginia to acquire a tract of land ten miles square situated on the Potomac River, as the site for a national capital. The ten miles, laid out in a square but set 45° to the cardinal points of the compass, became the actual seat of the government in 1800. However, in 1846 the third of the original grant that was situated in Virginia and included the community of Arlington, plus most of Alexandria, was receded to Virginia, thus accounting for the present odd shape of the District of Columbia. Interestingly, the precedent of the original charter of Maryland resulted in the placing of the District's southern boundary at the limit of *high water mark* on the *south bank* of the Potomac.

Until perhaps 1900, nearly all functions of the Federal Government and most of its personnel were accommodated easily within the confines of the District, but the tremendous expansion of the 20th century, accelerating phenomenally in World War II and continuously since, has far exceeded these limits so that now many federal agencies operate outside the District, and far more government employees reside without than within its boundary. This includes all operations in Virginia and those in such important Maryland communities as Silver Spring, Bethesda, College Park, Beltsville, among others. Indeed, numerous important federal operations have been dispersed as far as Baltimore (Social Security center) and Philadelphia (Internal Revenue center), not to mention many distant federal complexes, such as the Centers in Denver, Menlo Park, etc. In fact, there is probably no state without at least one, and many with numerous offices of the federal structure, in addition, of course, to the ubiquitous post offices. The District of Columbia has a population of three quarters of a million, but the surrounding urban complex is two or three times that figure.

This situation in and near Washington produces many inequities and is operationally cumbersome. The District is governed by the Congress, which is an egregious waste of valuable time that should be given to more vital concerns. Its citizens have no voice in local matters but vote only in national elections and have a voice but no vote in the Congress. The District collects no income tax from the many thousands of federal employees who work there and use its facilities, but live outside in Maryland or Virginia, where they pay their taxes but at least can vote on local matters. Crime laws applicable to the District, such as gun control, are ineffective because they do not apply outside. Low taxes on liquor (to accommodate Congressmen?) actually promote crime and lead to tax evasion or outright bootlegging. Admittedly these situations constitute acute social problems somewhat distinct from that of revamping the structure of the states. Nevertheless, they have implications of national import.

When the seat of government was placed in Washington, its location and conception were felicitous—far more so than for most of the colonial-born edifices it was to serve. It was geographically centered in the new country, with good accessibility for that period, by land or water, from north or south, and at a strategic point of departure for the still almost-unknown West.

But as we see it now, isn't it time to rethink this situation and ask if it were not better to readjust to the astonishingly different conditions of the present day and start over on a scale to match at least present needs and possibly those of some few future decades? Why not a new national capital somewhere nearer the present center of the country? Anywhere between Cincinnati and Denver east-west, and from Little Rock to Minneapolis north-south, would be a great improvement geopolitically. How about a hundred-mile square in the vicinity of Springfield, Missouri, for instance? Centrally situated on a well-watered rolling upland, readily accessible by road, rail or air, though not by water, this would likewise fit neatly between the proposed superstates of Iowa and Arkansa. Perhaps it should be surrounded by a Berlin-type wall to make sure all Federal activities and effects were confined within. Well, not really. If the hundred-mile square were adopted it probably would serve the purpose, but anything less might invite an early repetition of the problems just enumerated for the present District.

What to do with the existing federal complex in Washington? Perhaps it could be adapted for the capital of Chesapeak and otherwise become a glorified Williamsburg shrine. The example of Brasilia shows that such a change is not impossible. The advantages with respect to convenience for the assembly of the Congress and federal operatives, as well as from the standpoint of vulnerability to hostile attack, are obvious. Perhaps a more practical suggestion would be to permit it simply to subside into a major eastern federal center comparable to those already mentioned. In any case, the writer scarcely expects this plan to be effectuated tomorrow.

Nevertheless, the idea is worth pondering. It might suddenly become very pertinent if Washington, D.C., were obliterated in a moment by an atom bomb, which is no idle speculation.

LIABILITIES AND HAZARDS
OF REORGANIZATION

Admittedly the proposed restructuring of the nation would involve uncertainties and problems of its own, though surely nothing like those that faced the founders of the country in the first place, since there is now a vital going concern to work with and many useful precedents to suggest methods of operation that should be adopted and improved or avoided as undesirable. Perhaps one of the major objections likely to be raised is that the proposed superstates would be too powerful and might threaten to secede or disrupt the national unity if thwarted in individual courses that might run counter to national desires or objectives. This problem, however, is scarcely different from that the nation has faced and survived in the past. Surely not more than 2 or 3 of the thirteen proposed states would ever be sufficiently united at one time in pursuit of sectional desires or goals to challenge the national supremacy. Obvious regional blocks might be Mohawk and Chesapeak; Cherokee and Arkansa, plus Texas on occasion; Iowa and Ohio, with possibly Michigan in some circumstances; Arizona and Calvada, with only occasional cooperation from Texas, Dakota or Oregon; and possibly Dakota and Oregon in limited situations. Surely no single sectional interest would be a serious threat to the whole, and Alaska plus Hawaii would provide some stabilizing influence.

One minor complication surely would arise from the duplication of names, particularly of cities, towns and counties, within the proposed superstates. A casual check of the forty-eight states reveals twenty-five Springfields ranging from Springfield, Mass., (population 165,905) to Springfield, N. H., (pop. 310). Incidentally, both of these, plus Springfield, Maine, (pop. 336) would fall within the superstate of Merimak. There should be no difficulty in finding suitable substitute names, perhaps much more appropriate, for the two lesser Springfields. So also with the twenty-three Franklins, eighteen Jacksons, seventeen Washingtons, ten Columbias, eight Columbuses, and so on.

Counties involve even more duplication. There appear to be at least 31 Washington counties in the forty-eight states, as well as 26 Jeffersons, 23 Lincolns and 20 Madisons, plus numerous Monroes, Grants, Columbias, Adamses, etc. The combination of Franklin, Jackson, Jefferson, Lincoln, Madison and Washington seems to recur in some nine states. Perhaps some of these counties now would be glad to honor more recent presidents, such as Roosevelt or Eisenhower. Incidentally, the disparity in number of counties within presently constituted states is as absurd as many of their other comparative statistics, ranging from three in Delaware and eight in Conecticut to 254 in Texas. In population they vary from 7,032,075 for Los Angeles County, Cal., to only a few hundred for several counties in the semiarid west, such as Arthur, Neb., 606, and Dagget, Utah, 666. Certainly the county organization of existing states, or of proposed superstates, deserves thorough overhauling, but that is another project best left to the localities concerned.

CONCLUSION

The author is under no delusion that the suggestions offered are likely to be adopted soon, if ever, even in modified form, unless it should happen through violent revolution from within or complete defeat and destruction from without—both of which loom as hideous possibilities, however remote they may seem. Too many vested interests are at stake, each willing to fight to the death for its favored position at the feedtrough regardless of the damage it may do to the overall well-being. Unfortunately, there is little historical precedent in modern times for this type of governmental evolution to fit the changing circumstances. Italy was reconstituted after World War II by regrouping its 91 provinces into 19 operational regions which reflect local geography to a fair degree. France, after the revolution in 1789-91, reorganized its ancient provinces into 90 administrative departments, but these now are woefully unequal in population and importance, and are but poorly adjusted to geographic situations. Russia since the Bolshevik Revolution has become a union of fifteen socialist republics; but the R.S.P.S.R., centered on Moscow, with 75 per cent of the area and 60 per cent of the population, is completely dominant. The other republics, however, are fairly well tailored to fit ethnic groups, but with only accidental relationship to geography. Europe, unfortunately, is saddled with the results of centuries of history during which many ethnic groups differing greatly in language and cultural inheritance were evolved. Although most of these originally had some significant relationship to geography, rivalry and war have mangled these relationships, with disastrous results over most of central Europe. Only the peninsulas, such as Spain, Italy, Scandinavia, and the isolated British Isles, have been able to preserve any meaningful relationship to geography. The United States suffers no such sad inheritance, and is reasonably free from uncontrollable ethnic pressure; so that it is much more happily situated for reorganization into efficient administrative units.

In the proposed reconstitution, nine of the thirteen super-states would enjoy a share of the ocean front, with access to foreign trade. Two others (plus Mohawk) would divide the shores of our inland sea, the Great Lakes, with indirect access to the Atlantic. Only one state, Dakota, would be completely land-locked, although Ohio would have only river-way access to the sea. Generally, each state would be geographically diversified, with an important segment of low-lying, reasonably flat terrain suitable for residences, agriculture, industry and commerce, bordering on or near its coasts; and a more rugged or mountainous interior, pro-viding large areas of forest, in most cases with a variety of mineral resources, and as a rule providing excellent facil-ities for recreation. Above all, this hinterland would, in most cases, be its invaluable source of pure water, to be jealously guarded, carefully utilized, and justly apportioned to its more populous lowland. No state would be monoto-nous topographically, restricted economically and agricul-turally (and hence culturally), and devoid of any control over these conditions, as many of our present poorly en-dowed subdivisions are now. Each one could be proudly self-sufficient, yet each with a distinctive geographic and cultural identity unduplicated by any other.

In reply to the many objections that undoubtedly will be advanced against the thesis here presented, it is suggested that the objectors stop for a moment and contemplate what their attitude would be if the proposed reorganization actually were in existence and they had grown accustomed to it. Would anyone remotely consider carving up the thirteen great, proud self-sufficient commonwealths here proposed into forty-eight units, at least half of which were nothing more than miserable little jigsaw-puzzle pieces, and most of the remainder simple children's building-blocks?

SUMMATION

Map No. 10 and Table XV summarize the main features of this suggested plan for reorientation of the political structure of the United States heartland. No proposed superstate would contain more than one-eighth of the total population and none less than 2.2 per cent, a maximum variation of approximately five to one, compared to the present sixty to one (Table I, California to Wyoming). The greatest disparity in area would be reduced from 220 to one (Texas to Rhode Island) to only ten to one for Dakota-Mohawk. Even the density per square mile would be narrowed from a present 781, in Rhode Island, to less than one-fourth as much for the expanded area of Merimak, a situation that should tend to ease the suffocation of Rhode Islanders by giving them more room for political maneuvering within a hospitable framework. Conversely, the citizens of sparsely populated Nevada (five per square mile) should benefit in the long run from their increased freedom to operate in the expanded structures of more richly endowed Calvada or Arizona.

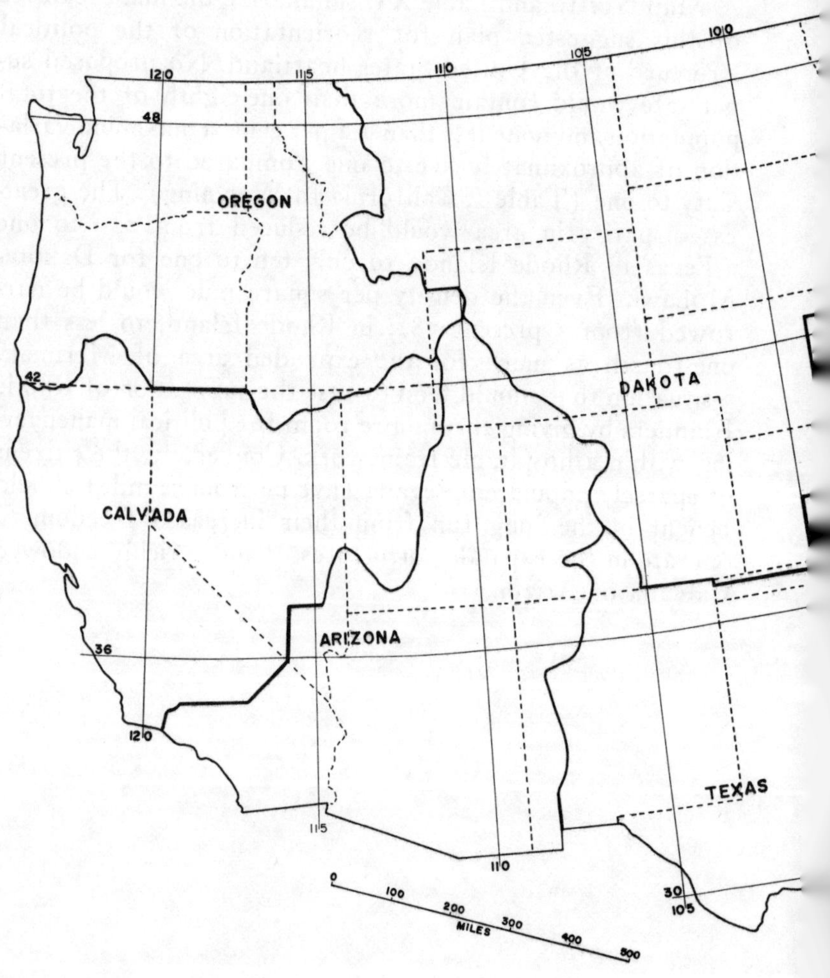
OREGON
DAKOTA
CALVADA
ARIZONA
TEXAS
120
115
110
105
100
48
42
36
30
0
100
200
300
400
500
MILES

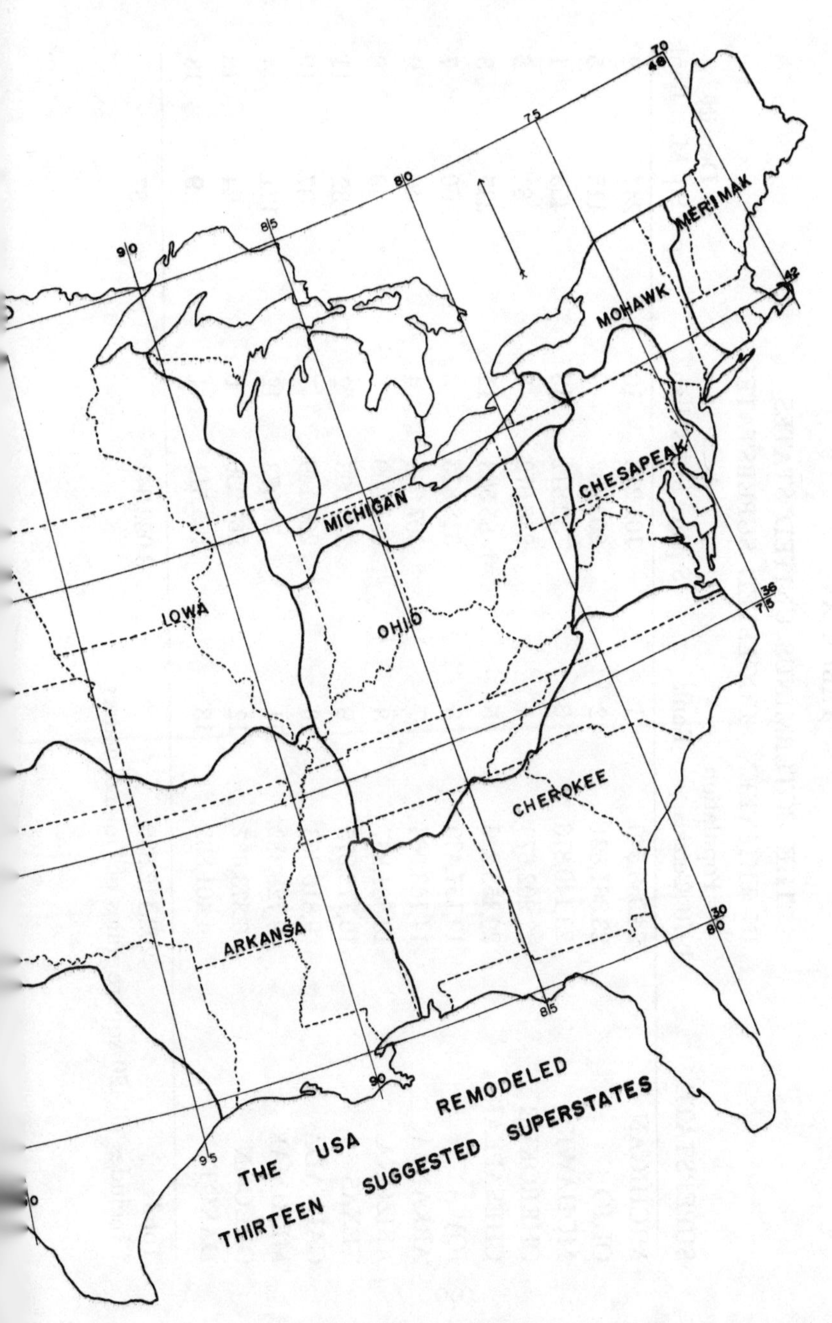
MERIMAK
MOHAWK
CHESAPEAK
MICHIGAN
IOWA
OHIO
CHEROKEE
ARKANSA
THE USA REMODELED
THIRTEEN SUGGESTED SUPERSTATES

TABLE XV

THE COTERMINUS UNITED STATES
IN THIRTEEN SUGGESTED SUPERSTATES

SUPERSTATE	Population 1970 Census	Rank	Area Square Miles	Rank	Density per Sq. M.	Rank
MICHIGAN	24,958,540	1	101,216	10	247	2
OHIO	23,361,821	2	203,932	9	115	5
MOHAWK	23,140,876	3	50,811	13	455	1
CHEROKEE	22,202,679	4	246,672	8	81	6
CHESAPEAK	20,153,226	5	85,588	11	235	3
IOWA	19,157,430	6	318,813	3	60	7
ARKANSA	14,163,064	7	307,538	4	46	9
ARIZONA	13,881,837	8	281,909	5	49	8
TEXAS	10,772,975	9	340,005	2	32	11
CALVADA	9,816,303	10	266,149	7	37	10
MERIMAK	9,728,382	11	56,973	12	171	4
OREGON	6,373,687	12	267,230	6	24	12
DAKOTA	4,401,866	13	495,511	1	9	13
Totals	202,112,686		3,022,347*		67	

* Includes 48,420 square miles of "inland waters."

APPENDIX

For those who may be interested in examining more closely the details of the partitions used in construction of the suggested superstates, the following tabulations are appended. Since thirteen existing states are included within various superstates in their entirety, their basic statistics are given in Table XVI. Data for the remaining thirty-five follow alphabetically. In general, the minor part of a state that has been separated for inclusion in a superstate is identified by counties, or occasionally fractions of a county, using 1970 census figures for county populations, with simple estimates for fractional portions. The usually larger remainder of the state assigned to a bordering superstate has been obtained by subtraction. Naturally, drainage divides do not coincide perfectly with county boundaries; but in most cases the differences are minor and should average out. It may be noted that the areas given for each state include that listed in census statistics as "inland waters," exclusive, however, of the United States portion of the Great Lakes. The amount of such "inland waters" averages out to about one and one-half percent, but varies from less than 100 to more than 4,000 square miles in various instances, and is shown in parentheses.

TABLE XVI
UNDIVIDED STATES

	Population—1970	Area—Square Miles	
Arizona	1,772,482	113,909	(334)
Arkansas	1,923,295	53,104	(429)
Delaware	548,104	2,057	(79)
Florida	6,789,443	58,560	(4298)
Iowa	2,825,041	56,290	(245)
Louisiana	3,643,180	48,523	(3361)
Maine	993,663	32,215	(2175)
Michigan	8,875,083	58,216	(1194)
New Hampshire	737,681	9,304	(287)
North Dakota	617,761	70,665	(608)
Rhode Island	949,723	1,214	(156)
South Carolina	2,590,516	31,055	(750)
Washington	3,409,169	68,192	(1406)

Alabama

Population, 3,444,165. Area, 52,169 (1091) square miles. Counties, 67.

To OHIO: Lauderdale (68,111), Limestone (41,699), Jackson (39,302), Franklin (23,933), Lawrence (27,281), Morgan (77,306), Marshall (54,211), DeKalb (41,981).

Total, 373,724. Approximate area, 10,000 square miles.

To CHEROKEE (residue): Population, 3,070,441. Area, 42,169 square miles.

California

Population, 19,953,134. Area, 158,693 (1953) square miles. Counties, 158.

To ARIZONA: Riverside (459,074), Imperial (74,-492), San Diego (1,357,854), Los Angeles (7,032,075), Ventura (376,430), Orange (1,420,386), San Bernardino (684,072).

Total, 11,404,383. Approximate area, 40,000 square miles.

To CALVADA (residue): Population, 8,548,751. Area, 118,693 square miles.

Colorado

Population, 2,207,259. Area, 104,247 (325) square miles. Counties, 63.

To ARIZONA: Archuleta (2,733), La Plata (19,199), Montezuma (12,952), Dolores (1,641), San Miguel (1,949), San Juan (831), Ouray (1,546), Gunnison (7,578), Montrose (18,366), Mesa (54,374), Delta (15,286), Pitkin (6,185),

Garfield (14,821), Eagle (7,498), Rio Blanco (4,842), Grand (4,107) Park (2,185), Jackson (1,811), Routt (6,592), Moffatt (6,525).

Total, 191,021. Approximate area, 35,000 square miles.

To TEXAS: Costilla (3,091), Alamosa (11,422), Saguache, mainly (3,500 est.), Mineral (786), Rio Grande (10,494), Conejos (7,846).

Total, 37,139. Approximate area, 4,000 square miles.

To DAKOTA (residue): Population, 1,979,099; Area, 65,247 square miles.

Connecticut

Population, 3,032,217. Area, 5,009 (110) square miles. Counties, 8.

To MOHAWK: Fairfield (792,814), Litchfield (N. W. corner) (125,000 est.), New Haven (744,948).

Total, 1,662,762. Approximate area, 2,009 square miles.

To MERIMAK (residue): Population, 1,369,455. Area, 3,000 square miles.

Georgia

Population, 4,589,575. Area, 58,876 (393) square miles. Counties, 159.

To OHIO: Dade (9,910), Catoosa (28,271), Fannin (13,357), Union (6,811), Towns (4,565), Walker, N ½ (25,000 est.).

Total, 87,914. Approximate area, 1,200 square miles.

To CHEROKEE (residue): Population, 4,501,661. Area, 57,676 square miles.

Idaho

Population, 713,008. Area, 83,557 (788) square miles. Counties, 44.

To CALVADA: Franklin (7,373), Bear Lake (5,801), Oneida (2,864).

Total, 16,038. Approximate area, 3,000 square miles.

To OREGON (residue): Population, 696,970. Area, 80,557 square miles.

Illinois

Population, 11,113,976. Area, 56,400 (465) square miles. Counties, 102.

To OHIO: Vermillion (97,047), Champaign, E. ½ (82,-000 est.), Douglas, E. ½ (10,000 est.), Edgar (21,591), Coles (47,815), Clark (16,216), Cumberland (9,772), Effingham (24,608), Jasper (10,741), Crawford (19,824), Clay (14,735), Richland (16,829), Lawrence (17,522), Wayne (17,004), Edwards (7,090), Wabash (12,841), Hamilton (8,665), White (17,312), Saline (25,721), Gallatin (7,418), Pope (3,857), Hardin (4,914), Johnson (7,550), Massac (13,889).

Total, 514,961. Approximate area, 9,500 square miles.

To MICHIGAN: Cook (5,492,369), Boone (25,440), McHenry (111,555), Lake (382,638), Kane (251,005), Du Page (491,882), Will (249,498), Iroquois (33,532), Kankakee (97,250), Grundy (26,535), Kendall (26,374), De Kalb (71,654).

Total, 7,259,732. Approximate area, 7,000 square miles.

To ARKANSA: Union (16,071), Pulaski (8,741), Alexander (12,015).

Total, 36,827. Approximate area, 1,000 square miles.

To IOWA (residue): Population, 3,302,456. Area, 38,900 square miles.

Indiana

Population, 5,193,669. Area, 36,291 (86) square miles. Counties, 92.

To MICHIGAN: Lake (546,253), Porter (87,114), La Porte (105,342), St. Joseph (245,045), Elkhart (126,529), La Grange (20,890), Noble (31,382), Steuben (20,159), Newton (11,606), Jasper (20,429), Starke (19,280), Benton, N ½ (5,000 est.).

Total, 1,239,029. Approximate area, 7,500 square miles.

To OHIO (residue): Population, 3,954,640. Area, 28,791 square miles.

Kansas

Population, 2,249,071. Area, 82,276 (168) square miles. Counties, 105.

To DAKOTA: Phillips (7,888), Rooks (7,628), Ellis (24,730), Tiego (4,436), Graham (4,751), Norton (7,279), Decatur (4,988), Sheridan (3,859), Gove (3,940), Logan (3,814), Thomas (7,501), Rawlins (4,393), Cheyenne (4,256), Sherman (7,792), Wallace (2,215), Greely (1,819), Hamilton (2,747), Stanton (2,287), Morton (3,576), Stevens (4,198), Grant (5,961), Kearney (3,047), Wichita (3,274), Scott (5,606), Lane (2,707), Finney (18,947), Gray (4,516), Meade (4,912), Seward (15,744), Haskell (3,672), Ford, W. ⅓ (15,000 est.).

Total, 197,483. Approximate area, 28,000 square miles.

To IOWA: Smith (6,757), Jewell (6,099), Republic
(8,498), Washington (9,249), Marshall (13,139), Nemaha
(11,825), Brown (11,685), Doniphan (9,107), Atchison (19,-
165), Leavenworth (53,340), Wyandotte (186,845), Jefferson (11,945), Jackson (10,342), Pottawatamie (11,755),
Riley (56,788), Clay (9,890), Cloud (13,466), Ottawa
(6,183), Mitchell (8,010), Lincoln (4,582), Osborne (6,416),
Russell (9,428), Ellsworth (6,146), Saline (46,592), McPherson, N. ½ (13,000 est.), Dickenson (19,993), Geary (28,111),
Wabaunsee (6,397), Shawnee (155,322), Osage (13,352),
Douglas (57,932), Johnson (217,662), Franklin (20,007),
Miami (19,254), Anderson (8,501), Linn (7,770), Bourbon
(15,215).

Total, 1,119,768. Approximate area, 27,000 square miles.

To ARKANSA (residue): Population, 931,820. Area,
27,276 square miles.

Kentucky

Population, 3,219,311. Area, 40,395 (531) square miles.
Counties, 120.

To ARKANSA: Carlisle (5,354), Hickman (6,264), Fulton (10,183), Graves (30,939).

Total, 52,740. Approximate area, 1,000 square miles.

To OHIO: (residue): Population, 3,166,571. Area, 39,-
395 square miles.

Maryland and District of Columbia

Population, 4,678,909. Area, 10,647 (696) square miles.
Counties, 23 plus Baltimore City (and District of Columbia).

To OHIO: Garrett, W. 2/3 (10,000 est.) Approximate area, 500 square miles.

To CHESAPEAK (residue): Population, 4,668,909. Area, 10,147 square miles.

Note: Includes 756,510 population and 70 square miles for District of Columbia.

Massachusetts

Population, 5,689,170. Area, 8,257 (390) square miles. Counties, 14.

To MOHAWK: Berkshire, ex. E. fraction (149,402). Approximate area, 857 square miles.

To MERIMAK (residue): Population, 5,539,768. Area, 7,400 square miles.

Minnesota

Population, 3,805,069. Area, 84,068 (4,059) square miles. Counties, 87.

To DAKOTA: Kittston (6,853), Roseau (11,569), Marshall (13,060), Pennington (13,266), Red Lake (5,388) Polk (34,453), Norman (10,008), Mahnomen (5,638), Clay (46,585), Becker, W. ⅓ (8,000 est.), Wilkin (9,389), Clearwater (8,013), Ottertail, W. ⅓ (16,000 est.).

Total, 188,222. Approximate area, 20,000 square miles.

To IOWA (residue): Population, 3,616,847. Area, 64,068 square miles.

Mississippi

Population, 2,216,912. Area, 47,716 (468) square miles. Counties, 82.

To OHIO: Tishomingo (19,940), Alcorn (27,179).

Total, 47,119. Approximate area, 1,000 square miles.

To CHEROKEE: Noxubee (14,288), Oktibenna (28,-752), Lowndes (49,700), Clay (18,840), Monroe (34,043), Itawba (16,847), Prentiss, E. ½ (10,000 est.).

Total, 172,470. Approximate area, 5,500 square miles.

To ARKANSA (residue): Population, 1,997,323. Area, 41,216 square miles.

Missouri

Population, 4,677,399. Area, 69,674 (448) square miles. Counties, 114 plus city of St. Louis.

To ARKANSA: Jasper (79,852), Newton (32,901), McDonald (12,357), Barry (19,597), Lawrence (24,585), Christian (15,124), Stone (9,921), Taney (13,023), Ozark (6,226), Douglas (9,268), Texas, E ⅓ (6,000 est.), Howell (23,521), Oregon (9,180), Shannon (7,196), Reynolds (6,106), Carter (3,878), Ripley (9,803), Butler (33,529), Wayne (8,546), Iron (9,529), Madison (8,641), Bollinger (8,820), Stoddard (25,771), Dunklin (33,742), Pemiscot (26,373), Scott (33,-250), Cape Girardeau (49,350), New Madrid (23,420), Mississippi (16,647).

Total, 566,156. Approximate area, 23,000 square miles.

To IOWA (residue): Population, 4,111,243. Area, 46,-674 square miles.

Montana

Population, 694,409. Area, 147,138 (1,260) square miles. Counties, 56.

To OREGON: Ravalli (14,409), Granite (2,737), Powell (6,660), Missoula (58,263), Mineral (2,958), Sanders (7,093), Lake (14,445), Flathead (39,460), Lincoln (18,063), Deer Lodge (15,652), Silver Bow (41,981).

Total, 221,721. Approximate area, 20,000 square miles.

To DAKOTA (residue): Population, 472,688. Area, 127,138 square miles.

Nebraska

Population, 1,483,791. Area, 77,227 (564) square miles. Counties, 43.

To DAKOTA: Sioux (2,034), Dawes (9,693), Box Butte (10,094), Sheridan (7,285), Cherry (6,846), Brown (4,021), Rock (2,231), Loup (991), Blaine (847), Thomas (954), Hooker (939), Grant (1,019), Logan (991), McPherson (623), Arthur (606), Garden (2,929), Morrill (5,813), Scott's Bluff (36,432), Banner (1,034), Kimball (6,009), Cheyenne (10,778), Deuel (2,717), Keith (8,487), Perkins (3,423), Lincoln (29,538), Custer (14,092), Dawson (19,467), Phelps (9,553), Gosper (2,178), Frontier (3,982), Hayes (1,530), Chase (4,129), Dundy (2,926), Hitchcock (4,051), Red Willow (12,191), Furnas (6,897), Harlan (4,357).

Total, 241,687. Approximate area, 45,000 square miles.

To IOWA (residue): Population, 1,242,104. Area, 32,-227 square miles.

New Jersey

Population, 7,168,164. Area, 7,836 (314) square miles. Counties 21.

To CHESAPEAK: Camden (456,291), Cape May (59,-554), Atlantic (175,043), Cumberland (121,374), Salem (60,346), Gloucester (172,681), Burlington (323,132), Mercer (303,968), Middlesex, W. side (40,000 est.), Hunterdon (69,718), Morris, W. ¼ (75,000 est.), Warren (73,879), Sussex (77,528), Somerset (198,372).

Total, 2,206,886. Approximate area, 5,236 square miles.

To MOHAWK (residue): Population, 4,961,278. Area 2,600 square miles.

New Mexico

Population, 1,016,000. Area, 121,666 (155) square miles. Counties, 32.

To ARIZONA: Hidalgo (4,734), Grant (22,030), Catron (2,198), Valencia, W. ⅓ (1,000 est.), McKinley (43,208), San Juan (52,517), Rio Arriba, W. ⅓ (2,500 est.).

Total, 128,187. Approximate area, 18,000 square miles.

To TEXAS (residue): Population, 887,813. Area, 103,-666 square miles.

New York

Population, 18,190,740. Area, 49,976 (1632) square miles. Counties, 62.

To MICHIGAN: Chautauqua (147,305), Cattaraugas (81,666), Erie (1,113,491), Wyoming, W. ½ (20,000 est.). Total, 1,362,462. Approximate area, 3,000 square miles.

To CHESAPEAK: Broome (221,814), Chenango (46,-368), Otsego (56,181), Cortland (45,894), Tompkins (76,879), Tioga (46,513), Chemung (101,537), Steuben, ½, (75,000 est.), Delaware (44,718), Sullivan (52,580).

Total, 767,484. Approximate area, 7,000 square miles.

To MOHAWK (residue): Population, 16,060,794. Area, 39,976 square miles.

Nevada

Population, 488,738. Area, 110,540 (751) square miles. Counties, 17.

To OREGON: Elko, N. ¼ (1,000 est.), Area, 3,000 square miles.

To ARIZONA: Clark (273,288), Lincoln, mostly (2,000 est.), Nye, fraction (1,000 est.).

Total, 276,288. Approximate area, 10,000 square miles.

To CALVADA (residue): Population, 211,450. Area, 97,540 square miles.

North Carolina

Population, 5,082,059. Area, 52,712 (3615) square miles. Counties, 100.

To OHIO: Cherokee (16,330), Clay (5,180), Graham (6,562), Macon (15,788), Swan (7,861), Jackson (21,593), Transylvania (19,713), Haywood (41,710), Henderson (42,-

804), Buncombe (145,056), Madison (16,003), Yancy (12,-629), Mitchell (13,447), Avery (12,655), Watauga (23,404), Ashe (19,571), Allegheny (8,134).

Total, 428,440. Approximate area, 7,000 square miles.

To CHEROKEE (residue): Population, 4,653,619. Area, 45,712 square miles.

Ohio

Population, 10,652,017. Area, 41,222 (422) square miles. Counties, 88.

To MICHIGAN: Williams (33,669), Defiance (36,949), Paulding (19,939), Putnam (31,134), Henry (27,058), Fulton (33,071), Lucas (484,370), Wood (89,722), Hancock (61,-217), Wyandot (21,826), Ashtabula (98,237), Seneca (60,-696), Sandusky (60,983), Ottawa (37,099), Erie (75,-909), Huron (49,587), Crawford (50,364), Lorain (256,843), Medina (82,717), Summit (553,371), Cuya-hoga (1,721,300), Geauga (62,977), Lake (197,200).

Total, 4,146,238. Approximate area, 10,000 square miles.

To OHIO (residue): Population, 6,505,779. Area, 31,-222 square miles.

Oklahoma

Population, 2,559,253. Area, 69,919 (888) square miles. Counties, 77.

To DAKOTA: Six-mile-wide strip on north edge of three Pandhandle counties, Beaver, Cimarron, Texas. Population, est. 3,000. Area, 1,000 square miles.

To TEXAS: Remainder of same three counties.

Population, 23,779. Area, 5,000 square miles.

To ARKANSA (residue): Population, 2,532,474. Area, 63,919 square miles.

Oregon

Population, 2,091,385. Area, 46,981 (666) square miles. Counties, 36.

To CALVADA: Klamath (50,021), Lake, S. ½ (4,000 est.).

Total, 54,021. Approximate area, 5,500 square miles.

To OREGON (residue): Population, 2,037,364. Area, 91,481 square miles.

Pennsylvania

Population, 11,793,909. Area, 45,333 (288) square miles. Counties, 67.

To MICHIGAN: Crawford (81,342), Erie (263,654).

Total, 344,996. Approximate area, 1,500 square miles.

To OHIO: Greene (36,090), Washington (210,876), Allegheny (1,605,016), Beaver (208,418), Butler (127,941), Mercer (127,175), Venango (62,353), Warren (47,682), McKean, W. ½ (25,000 est.), Forest (4,926), Elk, N.W. ⅔ (12,000 est.), Clarion (38,414), Jefferson (43,695), Armstrong (75,590), Indiana (79,451), Cambria (186,785), Westmoreland (376,935), Fayette 154,667), Clearfield, S.W. tip (1,000 est.).

Total, 3,424,014. Approximate area, 13,500 square miles.

To CHESAPEAK (residue): Population, 8,024,899. Area, 30,333 square miles.

Population, 666,257. Area, 77,047 (511) square miles. Counties, 67.

To IOWA: Roberts (11,678), Marshall, E. ½ (3,500 est.), Day (8,713), Grant (9,005), Codington (19,140), Hamlin (5,172), Deuel (5,686), Brookings (22,158), Kingsbury, E. ½ (3,000 est.), Lake (11,456), Moody (7,622), Miner, E. ½ (2,500 est.), McCook, E. ½ (4,000 est.), Minnehaha (95,209), Turner (9,872), Lincoln (11,761), Clay (12,923), Union (9,643).

Total, 253,038. Approximate area, 11,000 square miles.

To DAKOTA (residue): Population, 413,219. Area, 66,047 square miles.

Tennessee

Population, 3,924,164. Area, 42,244 (447) square miles. Counties, 95.

To ARKANSA: Lake (7,896), Obion (29,936), Weakley (28,827), Dyer (30,427), Gibson (47,871), Carroll (25,741), Henderson, W. ⅓ (6,000 est.), Madison (65,727), Crockett (14,402), Haywood (19,596), Lauderdale (20,271), Tipton (28,001), Shelby (722,014), Fayette (22,692), Hardemann (22,435), Chester (9,927), McNary. W. ⅓ (5,000 est.).

Total, 1,106,763. Approximate area, 8,500 square miles.

To OHIO (residue): Population, 2,817,401. Area, 33,744 square miles.

Texas

Population, 11,196,730. Area, 267,339 (3,826) square miles. Counties, 254.

To ARKANSA: Hardemann (6,795), Foard (2,211), Willbarger (15,355), Baylor (5,221), Wichita (121,862), Archer (5,759), Clay (8,079), Montague (15,326), Cooke (23,471), Grayson (83,225), Fannin (22,705), Lamar (36,-062), Red River (14,298), Bowie (67,813), Hunt (47,948), Hopkins (20,710), Titus (16,702), Cass (24,133), Van Zandt (22,155), Wood (18,589), Upshur (20,976), Harrison (44,-841), Marion (8,517), Smith (97,096), Rusk (34,102), Panola (15,894), Henderson, E. side (5,000), Anderson, E edge (10,000 est.), Nacogdoches (36,362), Sabine (7,187), Shelby (19,672), San Augustine (7,858), Angelina (49,349), Trinity, E. ½ (3,000 est.), Polk, N. ¼ (3,500 est.), Tyler (12,417), Jasper (24,692), Newton (11,657), Hardin (29,996), Jefferson (244,773), Orange (71,170), Houston, E. edge (4,000 est.), Cherokee (32,008).

Total, 1,372,486. Approximate area, 40,000 square miles.

To TEXAS (residue): Population, 9,824,244. Area, 227,339 square miles.

Utah

Population, 1,059,273. Area, 84,916 (2,577) square miles. Counties, 29.

To ARIZONA: Summit, E. side (1,000 est.), Dagget (666), Wasatch, S.E. corner (500 est.), Duchesne (7,299), Uintah (12,684), Carbon (15,647), Emery (5,137), Grand (6,688), San Pete, E. margin (500 est.), Sevier, E. end (1,000

est.), Wayne (1,483), Garfield, E. ¾ (1,000 est.), San Juan
(9,606), Kane (2,421), Washington (13,699).

Total, 79,330. Approximate area, 45,000 square miles.

To CALVADA (residue): Population, 979,943. Area,
39,916 square miles.

Vermont

Population, 444,732. Area, 9,609 (331) square miles. Counties, 14.

To MOHAWK: Bennington (29,282), Rutland (52,637),
Addison (24,266), Washington (47,659), Chittenden (99,-
131), Lamoille (13,309), Franklin (31,282), Orleans, W.
side (3,000 est.), Caledonia, W. tip (2,500 est.), Grand
Isle (3,574).

Total, 306,640. Approximate area, 5,769 square miles.

To MERIMAK (residue): Population, 138,092. Area,
3,840 square miles.

Virginia

Population, 4,648,494. Area, 40,815 (922) square miles.
Counties, 98.

To OHIO: Lee (20,321), Scott (24,376), Wise (35,947),
Smyth (31,349), Russell (24,533), Washington (40,835),
Tazewell (39,816), Dickenson (16,077), Buchanan (32,071),
Bland (5,423), Giles (16,741), Pulaski (29,564), Grayson
(15,439), Carroll (23,092), Floyd (9,775), Montgomery
(47,157).

Total, 412,516. Approximate area, 7,500 square miles.

To CHEROKEE: Patrick (15,282), Henry (50,901), Pittsylvania (58,789), Roanoke (67,339), Bedford (26,728), Campbell (43,319), Charlotte (11,551), Prince Edward (14,-379), Luneberg (11,687), Mecklenberg (29,426), Nottaway (14,260), Dinwiddie (25,046), Brunswick (16,172), Greenville (9,604), Sussex (11,464), Southampton (18,582).

Total, 424,529. Appproximate area, 6,000 square miles.

To CHESAPEAK (residue): Population, 3,811,449. Area, 27,315 square miles.

West Virginia

Population, 1,744,237. Area, 24,080 (101) square miles. Counties, 55.

To CHESAPEAK: Pendleton (7,031), Grant (8,607), Hardy (8,855), Mineral (23,109), Hampshire (11,710), Morgan (8,547), Berkeley (36,356), Jefferson (21,280).

Total, 125,495. Approximate area, 3,500 square miles.

To OHIO (residue): Population, 1,618,742. Area, 20,-580 square miles.

Wisconsin

Population, 4,417,933. Area, 56,154 (1449) square miles. Counties ,72.

To MICHIGAN: Iron, N. ½ (3,000 est.), Vilas, N. ½ (4,000 est.), Forest (7,691), Florence (3,298), Marinette (35,810), Langlade, E. ½ (10,000 est.), Menominee (2,607), Oconto (25,553), Shawano (32,650), Waupaca (37,780), Outagamie (119,356), Door (20,106), Brown (158,244), Kewaunee (18,961), Manitowoc (82,294), Calumet (27,604), Winnebago (129,931), Fond du Lac (84,567), Sheboygan

(96,660), Ozaukee (54,421), Washington (63,839), Dodge (69,004), Jefferson (60,060), Waukesha (231,365), Racine (170,838), Kenosha (117,917), Watworth (63,444).

Total, 1,731,000. Approximate area, 14,000 square miles.

To IOWA (residue): Population, 2,686,933. Area, 42,-154 square miles.

Wyoming

Population, 332,416. Area, 97,914 (408) square miles. Counties, 23.

To CALVADA: Uinta, W. 1/6 (5,100 est.), Lincoln, S.W. 1/4 (1,000 est.).

Total, 6,100. Approximate area, 1,500 square miles.

To OREGON: Lincoln, N. 1/4 (2,640 est.), Teton (4,823).

Total, 7,463. Approximate area, 4,000 square miles.

To ARIZONA: Uinta, 5/6 (2,000 est.), Lincoln, 1/2 (5,000 est.), Sublette (3,755), Sweetwater (18,391), Carbon, S.W. 1/8 (1,000 est.).

Total, 30,146. Approximate area, 20,000 square miles.

To DAKOTA (residue): Population, 288,707. Area, 72,414 square miles.